THE RISE AND FALL OF THE O'AHU KINGDOM

Mom
Remember
to live in the moment
and drink mai tais as
often as you can
Aloha! Mahalo
Happy 70th
Love Maryann

THE RISE AND FALL OF THE O'AHU KINGDOM

A BRIEF OVERVIEW
OF O'AHU'S HISTORY

ROSS CORDY

Mutual Publishing

Library of Congress Catalog Card
Number: 2002107045

ISBN 1-56647-562-7

Design by Jane Hopkins

First Printing, October 2002
1 2 3 4 5 6 7 8 9

Mutual Publishing
1215 Center Street, Suite 210
Honolulu, Hawaii 96816
Ph: (808) 732-1709 / Fax: (808) 734-4094
e-mail: mutual@lava.net / www.mutualpublishing.com

Printed in Australia by McPherson's Printing Group

Preface

THIS BOOK TAKES a different approach to the precontact history of the Hawaiian Islands. There are general archipelago models (e.g., Cordy 1974a, 1974b, 1978, 1981, 1992, Hommon 1976, 1986, 1992a, 1992b, Tuggle 1979, Kirch 1985, Spriggs 1988, Dye 1989, Kelly 1989, Burtchard 1992, Dye and Komori 1992). There are also several thousand contract archaeology reports which contain much information, but which rarely look beyond *ahupua'a* (community) patterns, if that far. Between are more recent studies of traditional districts: Halele'a (Earle 1973, 1978) and Nā Pali (Tomanari-Tuggle 1989) on Kaua'i; Wai'anae (Green 1980) and Waialua (Sahlins 1992) on O'ahu; Hāmākua (Cordy 1987a, 1994), Ka'ū (Cordy 1987b), and North Kohala (Tomonari-Tuggle 1981) on Hawai'i[1]. Of these, Green's Wai'anae study has had the greatest impact over the last decade. District studies enable a broader view of cultural patterns and changes than the *ahupua'a* level of analysis—a different and fascinating perspective. In late prehistory, however, districts were only portions of an Hawaiian polity, which usually approximated an entire major island. This book attempts an overview of a major island, hoping to gain some different viewpoints to move work forward on general patterns and changes in culture[2]. Oʻahu is the subject of analysis; the data are oral histories, the late 1700s to mid-1800s historical record, and archaeology.

Acknowledgments

This paper was first published in New Zealand in 1996 in a collection of papers presented to Professor Roger Green (Davidson, J.M., G. Irwin, B.F. Leach, A. Pawley, and D. Brown, editors. *Oceanic Culture History: Essays in Honour of Roger Green.* New Zealand Journal of Archaeology Special Publication.) Foss Leach and the New Zealand Journal of Archaeology kindly allowed this reprinting. The 1996 article is published here unchanged, except for the addition of photographs, some upgrading of diacritical marks on Hawaiian proper names, reformatting, and a few very rare word changes. Some words were spelled in British style in the original article and are left as they were. Thus, essentially this book is the same as the 1996 article. No editing to include new archaeological findings has been done.

My thanks to my colleagues for comments on a draft of the original 1996 paper: Tom Dye, Michael Kolb, Kana'i Kapeliela, Holly McEldowney, Eric Komori, Elaine Jourdane, and Dodie Lau. Thanks also to Marc Smith for the drafting work.

The
Environmental Setting[3]

O'AHU IS LOCATED at 157°18' W and 21°18' N. It is the third largest of the Hawaiian Islands, 1574 km², slightly smaller than Tahiti (2237 km²) in the Society Islands. O'ahu formed from two shield volcanoes, now eroded into two pinnacle-ridged, parallel mountain ranges, the 60 km long Ko'olaus and the 35 km long Wai'anaes, which reach high points of 946 m and 1227 m. Between these ranges is a 305 m high plateau in the center of the island. Terrain gradually descends on either side of this plateau. The mountains and plateau are surrounded by coastal plains up to 1.5-2.0 km wide. More recent eruptions have formed tuff and ash cones on the coastal plain, the most famous being Diamond Head or Lē'ahi on the south shore. The shore is fringed by white sand beaches, generally with low dunes.

The mountains and plateau are cut by streams into numerous valleys, 3.2-20.9 km in length, most being 4.8-9.7 km long. Valley widths are commonly up to 0.4-1.5 km. These upper valleys are steep-sided with narrow small stream flats; the lower valleys/coastal plains are much broader and flatter in slope. Deep alluvial soils and sands characterise the lower valleys and most of the coastal plains.

A fringing reef 0.5-2.0 km wide skirts the windward and southern sides of O'ahu, with depths of up to 9.1 m of water on the reef platform. The western shore has deeper waters in the lee; the northern shore has narrower reefs and is exposed to its famous winter waves. Two sizeable embayments with shallow calm waters are present: Kāne'ohe Bay on the eastern shore and Pearl Harbor (Pu'uloa) on the southern shore.

O'ahu is subject to northeast trade winds and orographic rainfall patterns. The northeast side of the island is the windward or wet side, receiving up to 1829 mm per year on the coast and 7620 mm on the ridges of the Ko'olaus. The leeward side of the Ko'olaus receives only 1524 mm in the mountain fringe and 508-762 mm on the shore. The leeward side of the Wai'anae Range is even drier, 1016 mm in the upper valley mountain fringes and 152 mm on the shore. Perennial streams flow heavily on the windward sides and less so on the leeward side of the Ko'olaus. Streams in the Wai'anaes tend to flow more consistently in the upper valleys and become intermittent near the shore.

At Polynesian settlement, the island was heavily vegetated. Windward coastal and lower valley forests were dominated by *Pandanus* spp. (*hala*) and *Pritchardia* palms (*loulu*), grading into an *'ōhi'a* (*Metrosideros polymorpha*) forest in mid-valleys, and then into an upper valley and mountain *'ōhi'a* forest mixed with giant tree fern (*Cibotium* spp.) (Beggerly 1990:277-78, 301, Hammatt *et al.* 1990, Athens and Ward 1991). The *'ōhi'a* forest continued over the Ko'olaus down through the leeward upper valleys. In the leeward lower valleys and coastal plains of the Koʻolaus, pollen cores have identified a dry-mesic forest (Wickler *et al.* 1991:52-55, Henry and Rosendahl 1993:23, 27, Appendix H; Denham *et al.* 1993:44). On the leeward-most side of the Waiʻanaes, an even drier forest is indicated, with remnant dry forests of *lama* (*Diaspyros sandwicensis*) or *āulu* (*Sapindus oahuensis*) on lower ridges (Cuddihy and Stone 1990) and with open forests on mid-lower valley floors and coastal plains dominated by *wiliwili* (*Erythrina sandwicensis*), *loulu*, and *ʻaʻaliʻi* (*Dodonaea*) (Nature Conservancy of Hawaii 1987, Charvet-Pond and Davis 1991:166-67, Scott-Cummings 1991).

In brief, 'There was nothing to complain of anywhere on Oʻahu—it was fertile in the uplands, fertile in the lowlands' (Kamakau 1991:68). As will be seen, this was a desirable land in wars of late prehistory. And, particularly in earlier times, Oʻahu's marked windward-leeward pattern affected the amount of available water and accordingly settlement.

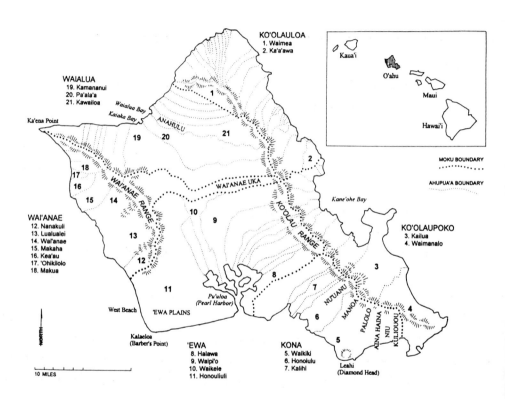

Figure 1: Places mentioned in the first part of this book.

Traditional Moku

AT EUROPEAN CONTACT (1779), the island was divided into six districts (*moku*), Koʻolaupoko, Koʻolauloa, Waialua, Waiʻanae, ʻEwa, and Kona, which were large land areas extending from the reefs up to the main ridge lines (Fig. 1). Each district contained between 6 and 31 communities or *ahupuaʻa* (cf. Hawaiian Studies Institute 1987). Koʻolaupoko and Koʻolauloa were windward districts. Koʻolauloa consisted of narrower valleys from Kaʻaʻawa to Waimea, most with narrow fringing reefs. Koʻolaupoko was encompassed by a 450 m high, fluted, cliff-face (*pali*) stretching around Kāneʻohe Bay and extending to the southeast end of the island. Koʻolaupoko included nine *ahupuaʻa* around Kāneʻohe Bay and the larger Kailua and Waimānalo *ahupuaʻa* to the east. Broad, flat lower valley floors and/or large coastal marshes characterise this district.

Kona covered the leeward, southeastern part of the island fronting the Koʻolaus. To the east of Diamond Head are short (3.2-4.8 km long) valleys and narrow coastal plains: Kuliʻouʻou, Niu, ʻĀina Haina. To the west of Diamond Head are larger, 6.4-8 km long valleys (Mānoa and Pālolo, Nuʻuanu, and Kalihi), which historically were the economic and demographic core of the district, with Waikīkī *ahupuaʻa*

Ca. 1786 View of Coastal Houses, likely in the Niu to Hawai'i Kai area. (From George Dixon 1789. *A Voyage Round the World...* London, George Goulding. Photo from Hawai'i State Archives.). These lands were in Kona District (moku), east of Waikīkī, and as drier, leeward lands, they were not permanently occupied until sometime between A.D. 1000-1300.

(with Mānoa-Pālolo) the political center. These larger valleys all emptied out on to a wide coastal plain.

To the west was leeward ʻEwa District. ʻEwa curved out from the Koʻolaus, across the central plateau, and encircled Pearl Harbor. Its population and production were centred on Pearl Harbor. Long, narrow valleys run out of the Koʻolaus and off the central plateau and empty on to small lower valley plains along Pearl Harbor. Hālawa (9.7 km long), Waipiʻo (14.5 km long), and Waikele (19.5 km long) are several of these valleys. Honouliuli (9 km long), the westernmost stream, originates in the Waiʻanaes. The far western area of ʻEwa, the ʻEwa Plain, is raised Pleistocene reef and was one of the island's driest areas.

The *moku* of Waiʻanae consisted of the extremely dry, western flank of the Waiʻanae Range. Here, wide amphitheatre-backed valleys are in the late stage of valley development, with thin, sometimes discontinuous ridges. Waiʻanae Valley, with the most perennial stream, was the political, economic and demographic center of this district. The *moku* had other large valleys (Lualualei, Nānākuli and Mākaha) and smaller valleys (Keaʻau, ʻŌhikilolo, Mākua). Larger valleys are about 6.4-8 km long. Waiʻanae also had a narrow land extension which crossed the central plateau from the Waiʻanaes to the Koʻolaus, called Waiʻanae uka.

Along the north shore of Oʻahu lay the sixth *moku*, Waialua. Here, two 18-21 km long stream drainages (Anahulu and Helemano- Poamoho-Kaukonahua) emerge from their narrow upper valleys which cut through the central plateau, empty on to a wide coastal plain, and enter the sea at Waialua and Kaiaka Bays. The focal economic and demographic *ahupuaʻa* of this district, Kamananui, Paʻalaʻa and Kawailoa, were located on this plain.

A.D. 0-900s

Early Settlement

A 1970s MODEL of Hawaiian cultural changes suggested that permanent settlement was first established on windward Oʻahu in the Koʻolauloa and Koʻolaupoko Districts (Cordy 1974a), and this concept has been widely accepted (Hommon 1976:232, 1986:67, Green 1980:71, Kirch 1985: Ch.5, Spriggs 1988:59). There, high rainfall and perennial streams supplied a consistent source of water for agriculture. Drought and crop losses were unlikely to occur, in contrast to the leeward side. The windward areas also had easy access to marine resources. Early settlement was suggested to have taken place about the A.D. 300s-600s (Newman 1972:561, Cordy 1974a, 1974b, Kirch 1974, Hommon 1976). The model further predicted that permanent settlement gradually expanded in windward areas and then spread to leeward lands (Cordy 1974a). For Oʻahu, it was stated that leeward areas with flowing, year-round streams (notably those around Pearl Harbor) may also have been permanently occupied fairly early, albeit after optimal windward areas. It was suggested that the drier leeward lands, such as those of Waiʻanae, were not permanently occupied until about A.D.

1100. This model is now 20 years old, and despite new information, it still seems to be supported, with settlement dates somewhat earlier and some striking anomalous dates.

Note, the model did not imply that the leeward lands of 'Ewa, Kona, Wai'anae and Waialua were unused. Important leeward resources (e.g., fishing grounds, clams and oysters in shallow Pearl Harbor, bird nesting areas, timber, and feather birds) were expected to have been used by people from the windward areas. As a result, a fair number of small, temporary camp-sites, whether caves or surface structures, should have been used.

Several sites have now been dated to early times in the *ahupua'a* of Waimānalo, Kailua and Kāne'ohe in windward Ko'olaupoko. One area is Bellows in Waimānalo. Here, streams drain off the *pali*, open on to swampy flats, and cross a coastal plain of undulating sand flats[4]. A long white sand beach with low dunes fringes the shore. The Bellows sites consist of multiple habitation layers in the coastal dune and on the sandy plain along Waimānalo's northernmost stream (Pearson *et al.* 1971, Cordy and Tuggle 1976, Shun 1992). Initial work in the dune found firepits and postholes; adzes and fishhooks of early types were recovered from lower layers. The first radiocarbon dates obtained were not precise, ranging from the A.D. 600s to 1200s[5]. Volcanic glass dates suggested occupation extended back to the A.D. 300s-500s (Kirch 1974, Cordy and Tuggle 1976, Tuggle *et al.* 1977). So do recently obtained radiocarbon dates. One from the inland edge of the coastal plain is A.D. 245-625 (Streck and Watanabe 1988), and another from near the dune is A.D. 940-1330 (Layer VIII), with a lower cultural layer (X) undated

(Miller 1989). Most researchers still accept an A.D. 300s-600s range for the initial occupation of the Bellows area, while realising that most site areas date from the A.D. 900s or later. Early occupation at the dune has been variously argued to be permanent habitation (Pearson *et al*. 1971) or temporary habitation (Cordy and Tuggle 1976, Beggerly 1990:149-51). It is suggested here that there was early permanent settlement in Waimānalo, at least near prime farming areas at the interface of the upper valleys and coastal plain, and maybe on the Bellows Dune.

Four sites in Kailua *ahupuaʻa* have early dates: 2022 (Bishop Museum site G6-32), 2023 (G6-33), 2131 (G6-70), and 2129 (G6-68). Kailua has several upper valleys (Maunawili, Kahanaiki, and Kapaʻa) which empty into a huge lower valley marsh (Kawainui). Kawainui in turn drains south around the flank of a solitary mountain peak, Olomana, and into another large marsh pond (Kaʻelepulu), and both are fronted by a wide curved beach berm along a calm bay with a wide reef. Site 2022 is on the slopes of Kawainui Marsh near the entry of Maunawili Stream. Recent work has identified a layer (II) up to 1 m thick containing scattered charcoal flecking, some hearths and artefacts (largely lithics). Two early dates were obtained of A.D. 770-1270 and 799-1256 (Erkelens 1993: 50), overlapping with one of two dates obtained more than 10 years before (A.D. 353-655 and 529-965, [Clark 1980:71, 77-79]). Most of the site reflects dryland gardening, but one area had hearths, food remains and artefacts which were interpreted as evidence of permanent settlement (Erkelens 1993:60). Site 2023, at the back of the marsh, is a small terrace interpreted as a temporary habitation site. It has a radiocarbon date of A.D. 706-898 (Clark 1980:72,

80). The remaining early dates come from two sites (2131 and 2129) in the mid-portions of Maunawili Valley. These were irrigated terraces which dated to A.D. 897-1260 and A.D. 980-1280, respectively (Allen pers. comm. 1993). These Kailua dates identify early permanent habitation and agriculture along the colluvial slopes at the back edge of the marsh and irrigated farming into the mid-portions of the upper valleys.

Early sites are also found in Kāneʻohe. Kāneʻohe is backed by the high *pali*, and on the sea it fronts the sheltered waters of Kāneʻohe Bay. Unlike Kailua, the lower valleys of the two streams in Kāneʻohe are relatively narrow, and the upper valley tributary system is more extensive. Early agricultural sites have been found in Luluku, 4 km inland at the base of the *pali*. Here, there is an A.D. 440-910 date from a possible irrigated terrace (site 1887 or G5-85) and an A.D. 915-1280 date from a dryfield terrace (1888, G5-86)(Allen *et al*. 1987:176, 229-30). Two early dates also come from habitation features in adjacent site 2038 (G5-106), A.D. 411-640 and 890-1149 (Williams 1989:20). These dates, from so far inland, suggest an already expanding windward population by the A.D. 500s-1000s (see also Allen 1992)[6].

Anomalous dates come from two areas in windward Koʻolauloa District. Work at Kahuku *ahupuaʻa* found habitation layers in a high coastal dune at Kahuku Point (site 2911). A radiocarbon date of B.C. 165-A.D. 210 was obtained from Layer V (since renumbered Layer IV)(Bath *et al*. 1984:53). Follow-up excavations obtained more dates from the lowest layers, but these only go back to the A.D. 1000s-1200s (Walker *et al*. 1988:89-91). These later workers state that the ʻearly date must now be viewed with considerable scepticism; however, it should not be totally rejected because it may reflect an isolated feature which predates the majority of the deposit' (Walker *et al.* 1988:113).

Also in Ko'olauloa is the 6.5 km long Kahana Valley. Recent work studied the change from embayment to marsh in the lower valley (Beggerly 1990). Cores in the marsh revealed marine lagoonal soils in Layer VI with washed-in terrestrial material: charcoal in sediments, *Pandanus* and *'ōhi'a* forest pollen, *Aleurites* (*kukui*) pollen, pollen of plants indicative of human disturbance of forests, and minimal *Cordyline* (*ki*) and *Colocasia* (*kalo*) pollen (Beggerly 1990:238, 309-13). One radiocarbon date of B.C. 430-30 was obtained from this layer (Beggerly 1990:309-13). Mucky peat (IV) and soils (III) marked the formation of the marsh, Layer IV having a date of A.D. 895-1255 (Beggerly 1990: 249-50). Shell samples associated with burials in the current beach berm have been radiocarbon dated to A.D. 770-1130 (500 year reservoir correction)(Beggerly 1990:244). A concern is whether the evidence of human presence in Layer VI is accurately dated. It is likely that this layer contains later terrestrial sediments mixed in with earlier marine sediments and that the date applies to the marine sediments (cf. Spriggs and Anderson 1993, Dye pers. comm.). Even the principal researcher urges caution, as only one sample from Layer VI is dated (Beggerly 1990:355). Other dates from the valley, however, clearly seem to show settlement by the A.D. 700s-1200s; burials and agricultural pollen suggest permanent habitation.

Early dates from the leeward side of O'ahu also have increased in numbers since the early 1970s. In 'Ewa District, a buried habitation deposit (site 3321) was found at the inland edge of the lower valley of Honouliuli, the westernmost stream of Pearl Harbor. The site is of moderate size (450 m²) with two thin layers, II and IV. These layers contained firepits, earth ovens, postholes, food remains, and some artefacts. Layer IV has a date of A.D. 540-880 (Dicks *et al*. 1987:45). Whether Layer IV is the remains of permanent or temporary occupation is still unclear and awaits clarification in the final excavation report.

Early dates also come from sites on the arid western fringe of the 'Ewa Plain in today's Ko Olina Resort (Davis *et al*. 1986:19-22, 25, Davis and Haun 1986, Charvet-Pond and Davis 1991:61, 75, 163-77, 179, Dunn *et al*. 1991:9). Here, a small stream from the nearby Wai'anae mountains emptied into an inland marsh, which in turn drained through flat limestone lands into a salt marsh behind narrow, low coastal dunes. Apparent human manipulation of the inland marsh's (site 3357) flora dates to at least A.D. 225-565. Backhoe trenches uncovered a buried habitation deposit (site 1446-1) at the base of the low limestone escarpment next to the marsh. This site has complex stratigraphy with overlapping firepits, midden deposits, and intervening non-cultural alluvium. Fishbone, shellfish, bird bone (flightless goose, etc.), early types of one-piece bone and pearlshell fishhooks, and basalt adze blanks of unusual and often early forms were found. This site yielded an initial use date of A.D. 145-600. Rockshelters (site 3355) in the escarpment across the marsh were also excavated, and deposits dated back to the A.D. 600s-1000s. Also, the coastal dune had subsurface deposits (site 1438-1) with one date of A.D. 410-660, but most post-1200s. The dune deposits contained food remains (fish, molluscs, sea birds and extinct geese), postholes, firepits and fishhooks of early type. The researchers concluded that these three sites reflected 'very dispersed' 'temporary encampments utilized by fishermen and bird collectors'.

The last of the early leeward sites identified so far is site 4000 (known as O1), a rockshelter at the tip of the ridge separating Niu and Kuli'ou'ou Valleys in Eastern Kona District. The site overlooks the narrow coastal plain of Kuli'ou'ou, with the beach only 183 m away. O1 is 16 m wide at its mouth, 8 m deep and 2.4 m high, with a covered living area of 39 m² (Emory and Sinoto 1961:5-6). The floor of the cave contained up to 1 m of deposits with multiple overlying fireplace ash lenses, numerous artefacts, and food remains (Emory and Sinoto 1961). The faunal material shows a typical pattern of early use with larger amounts of bird bone in the early deposits (Emory and Sinoto 1961:17, Dye and Steadman 1990). A date of A.D. 760-1320 was obtained from charcoal slightly up from the base of the deposits (Emory and Sinoto 1961:15). Multiple, overlapping firepits indicate that this was a temporary campsite, clearly used recurrently over the years.

Ignoring the two very early dates from Kahuku and Kahana which must await further evaluation, the above information points to a picture of initial settlement on O'ahu between A.D. 0-600. Despite recent questioning of the earliest Bellows dates (Spriggs pers. comm. 1991) and of the earliest South Point sand dune dates (Dye 1992), a number of sites dating between A.D. 0-900s are now appearing in the archaeological record and not just on O'ahu, but also on Hawai'i (more than 20 sites) and Kaua'i (four or more)[7]. Many researchers now consider a settlement date of about A.D. 0-300 for O'ahu and the other major islands to be very reasonable. The nature of early sites is still difficult to analyse, given small excavation samples. But the windward sites of O'ahu (Kāne'ohe, Kailua, Kahana) do seem to reflect more settled populations with associated agricultural sites[8]. Leeward sites at Ko Olina on the 'Ewa Plains and the O1 cave in Eastern Kona fit the pattern of small temporary campsites.

Most researchers assume that during this early period, political organization would have been in small polities with the Ancestral Polynesian primogeniture ranking and chiefly system, but with minimal hierarchical organization (e.g., Kirch 1973, 1984, Cordy 1974a, 1974b, 1978, 1981, 1985, Hommon 1976, 1986, 1992b, Spriggs 1988)—the patriarchical organization that Fornander (1919-20:252) deduced from his review of oral traditions. A number of small polities are expected to have existed in windward Ko'olauloa and Ko'olaupoko. Hommon (1976:230) suggested that these polities might be district-sized, which implies many communities within each polity. I believe the polities would have been smaller in size, judging from patterns of simple-ranked societies in Polynesia at European contact (e.g., Cordy 1981:39-44, 1985:160). Lands within the community would have been held by nonunilineal kin groups, and the territories are suggested to have extended inland up the valleys (Hommon 1986, 1992b:7). Hommon (1986, 1992b) has labelled the communities '*āina*' and the kin groups 'archaic *maka'āinana*'. The lands of Wai'anae, 'Ewa, Kona and Waialua may have been claimed by certain windward polities, or may have remained open[9]. On the basis of comparisons with similar simple-rank societies in Polynesia and Micronesia at European contact, these polities probably each had populations of no more than about 500-1500 (Cordy 1978, 1985:160). A chief and his kinsmen probably held the administrative positions, with minimal behavioural isolation from the rest of the population and with minimal secular power held by the chief—Fornander's time of minimal *kapu* (1880:63). Also, these small polities undoubtedly had religious structures, but they are expected to have been very small. As yet, no religious structures have been dated prior to the A.D. 1000s on Oʻahu, or on any of the Hawaiian Islands (Kolb 1991:247, 249).

A.D. 1000s-1300s
Settlement of the Leeward Lands of Oʻahu and
the Emergence of District-sized Polities

THE POPULACE OF the windward side appears to have
been intensifying and expanding their farm lands up the
valleys during these centuries. Dates from Kailua
(Koʻolaupoko) show continued cultivation and housing
along the marsh slopes (Erkelens 1993: cf.50), taro
pondfields built out into the marsh at the mouth of
Maunawili Stream in the A.D. 1200s-1300s (Allen-Wheeler
1981:63), irrigated terraces in the middle portions of
Maunawili (Allen pers. comm. 1993) and the initial spread
of dryland farms, irrigated terraces, and temporary camps
into upper Maunawili in the late A.D. 1200s-1400s (Mills
and Williams 1992:89-91, Allen pers. comm. 1993). In
Kāneʻohe (Koʻolaupoko), the inland Luluku terraced
pondfields became complex and extensive by the
mid-1200s (Allen et al. 1987: 230, 249). Adjacent field
shelters, marked by earth ovens, increased in numbers,
and inland permanent habitations appeared in the A.D.
1200s (Williams 1992).

The movement of permanent habitation to the
leeward side of Oʻahu took place by the A.D. 1000s-1100s.
By the 1300s, much of the island had become permanently

occupied, with at least the lower valley plains farmed. In 'Ewa, taro pondfields, indicative of associated permanent settlement, were in the lower valley of Honouliuli by the A.D. 1000s-1100s, and perhaps slightly earlier (Dicks *et al.* 1987:65, 74, 79, Davis *et al.* 1988, Davis 1990:18). Similar early farm lands and houses were quite probably present along the lower floodplains in other Pearl Harbor lands such as Hō'ae'ae, Waikele and Waipi'o. Indeed, in the easternmost *ahupua'a* of Pearl Harbor, Hālawa, permanent house sites and fields were scattered up the middle and upper reaches of north and south Hālawa valleys in the A.D. 1200s-1400s (Crozier 1972:28, Dye 1977:18, Spear 1991), suggesting settlement had begun even earlier on the fertile coastal plain. Pollen studies near the mouth of Hālawa Stream show that the coastal forest was being cleared about A.D. 890-1294 (a shell sample, *Pinctada radiata*, reservoir corrected, from just below the pollen sample studied, Denham *et al.* 1993:44).

In Kona District, pollen studies on the seaward flats of Kalihi found a rapid decline of extensive *Pritchardia* palm forests after A.D. 1000 (Wickler *et al.* 1991:52-55), probably indicating clearing for farming. Dates from mid-valley areas from the A.D. 1200s-1400s onwards are from agricultural sites in Kuli'ou'ou (Barrera 1979:6-12), from near a small *heiau* in Maunalua, Hawai'i Kai, (Davis and Kaschko 1980:3, Davis 1985:16), from permanent houses in Moanalua (Ayres 1970), from taro fields in Kalihi (Watanabe 1986), and from a deposit associated with burials in Waikīkī-Mānoa (Hammatt and Shideler 1991:40). The dates from these mid-valley areas support the idea that settlements and farms were nearer the shore at an earlier time, roughly the A.D. 1000s-1300s. Dates

Table 1
Rulers of O'ahu[10]

Estimated
Date

1300-1320		Māweke		
1320-1340	Muli'eleali'i	Keaunui		Kalehenui
1340-1360	Kumuhonua	Mō'īkeha		'Olopana
1360-1380	'Elepu'ukahonua	Ho'okamali'i		
1380-1400	Ho'okupohokano (Kahokupohakano)	Kaha'i		
1400-1420	Nāwele	Kūolono		
1420-1440	La'akona²	Ma'elo (f)		
1440-1460	Kapae-a-La'akona	Lāulihewa		
1460-1480	Huapouleilei	Kahuoi		
1480-1500	-	Pua'a a Kahuoi		
1500-1520	-	Kūkahia'ililani		
1520-1540	Haka	Mā'ilikūkahi		
1540-1560		Kalona-iki		
1560-1580		Piliwale		
1580-1600		Kūkaniloko (f)		
1600-1620		Kala'imanuia (f) (Kalanimanuia)		
1620-1640	Kū-a-Manuia	Ka'ihikapu-a-Manuia	Ha'o	Kekela (f)
1640-1660		Kākuhihewa ↘	Nāpūlānahumahiki	
			↘ Kaea-a-Kalona (f) (Ka-haiao-nui-aKaua'ilana)	
1660-1680		Kānekapu-a-Kākuhihewa		
1680-1700		Kaho'owahaokalani		
1700-1720		Kauakahi-a-Kaho'owaha		
1720-1740		Kuali'i (Ku-i-ke-ala-i-ka-ua-o-ka-lani)		
1740-1760	Kapi'iokookalani	Peleiōholani³ (d. 1779)		'Elani (d.1785)
1760-1780	Kanahaokalani	Kumuhana		
1780-1800		Kāneoneo (d. 1785)		Kahahana (d.1785)

(f) = Female

from Waikīkī show settlement was well established along the shore by the A.D. 1400s (Davis 1989:6, 25, 47-48, 77, 1991:67, Schilz 1991:3), suggesting settlement had begun several centuries earlier.

Waiʻanae District also became permanently occupied during these centuries (Green 1980). Waiʻanae Valley, watered by flowing streams and a large spring, may have been first settled (Green 1980:72). The sparse archaeological information available tends to suggest that in the 1000s-1300s the permanent dwellings of this *moku* were near the shore and the farms nearby or just inland. In Mākaha, dates from field shelters amidst dry fields fall into this time period (sites 17 and 18a, Area 776) (Green 1980:48). These field shelters are on the sides of the lower valley, in areas nearest the shore, which suggests that the permanent dwellings of the users of these shelters were in the coastal zones (Green 1980:72, 74). Archaeological work has shown that mid-valley and upper valley areas of Mākaha (Green 1980), Lualualei (Haun 1985) and Nānākuli (Cordy *et al.* n.d.) were not permanently occupied or farmed until the A.D. 1400s-1500s, supporting the view that settlement was focused more seaward a few centuries earlier.

Little work has occurred in Waialua, but excavations in the mid to upper portions of Anahulu Valley in Kawailoa *ahupuaʻa*, 5-11 km inland, found that agricultural and temporary habitations were present by the A.D. 1200s-1400s (Kirch and Spriggs 1993: 5-8), suggesting that permanent habitation along the coastal plain had begun earlier.

Oral histories show that at the end of this period, by the late A.D. 1200s or early 1300s, island-wide political changes were occurring. From this point on, the oral traditions of Oʻahu provide a crucial framework to help understand the remaining years of prehistory, with specifics keyed to certain rulers. Table 1 presents the genealogy of Oʻahu's rulers. An estimate of 20 years per generation has been used to date the ruling line, following the reasoning of Stokes (1933) and Cartwright (1930) and following Hommon (1976) and my prior work (Cordy 1987a).

The oral accounts document the formation of district-based polities, which I assume were larger than earlier polities, by the early 1300s. About A.D. 1320-1340, the sons of Māweke were in control over three powerful polities: ʻEwa, Kona, and Koʻolaupoko. ʻEwa was a supra-district polity, including three traditional districts, ʻEwa, Waiʻanae and Waialua (Fornander 1880:48), so the polities forming at that time did not simply correspond with the political districts of late prehistory[11]. The senior line of Māweke (the Māweke-Kumuhonua line) rose to prominence in these times, and was centred in the ʻEwa polity (Fornander 1880:68, 88). Kumuhonua of this line is said by some to have been nominal ruler of the island (Fornander 1880:49) about A.D. 1340-1360.

With a polity ruler in place over a district or several districts, more levels of chiefs were likely to be present— a complex-rank political organization—with at least local chiefs under the ruler. This organization presumably was kin-based, the ruler being the senior man in the dominant and putatively senior kin group (localised lineage), and his kinsmen and the heads of local ʻāina, dominant lineages, being the lower chiefs (cf. Earle 1978:168-70, Green 1980:72-73, 75). The land-holding system would also be based on the kin system, with local kin groups (archaic *maka'āinana*) controlling land (Hommon 1986). Polities may have held about 1000-3000 people, judging from similar patterns in Polynesia at European contact (Cordy 1978, 1985:160) and on estimates from 1800s Ka'ū (Hommon 1976:234).

The traditions about the late A.D. 1300s also emphasise greater separation of the chiefs from the commoners (Fornander 1880:63). There was reputedly stricter access to chiefly status; an 'Aha Ali'i council required proven ties to the ruler within 10 generations (Fornander 1880:28-30, 63, Kamakau 1991:42, 156). Temple worship was said to be more restricted to rulers and chiefs (Fornander 1880:59)[12]. Again, these changes are aspects of the formation of complex political organization.

Signs of these political changes should appear in the archaeological record. Major religious structures used by the rulers should have been built or rebuilt over older structures and perhaps have been larger in size[13]. *Heiau* size was probably fairly small, in view of archaeological excavations on Hawai'i and Maui Islands. On Hawai'i, the early building stage of 'Āle'ale'a *heiau*, which dated to the A.D. 1000s-1300s, was only 252 m² (Ladd 1969, 1987). Three *heiau* on Maui at this time were also small: Pihana (432 m²), Lanikele (304 m²), and Molohai (309 m²)(Kolb 1991:151, 167, 184). In contrast, Pōpōiwi *heiau* had an area of 1042 m² (Kolb 1991:178), so the construction of larger *heiau* did begin at some point in this period. No O'ahu *heiau* of defined sizes have yet been dated to this period. Kukuiokāne *heiau* in inland Kāne'ohe, a large *heiau* in late prehistory, saw some construction activity starting in the A.D. 1300s (Williams 1992) but the size of the structure then is not clear. Extrapolating from contact patterns, such major religious structures would be mostly expected at the ruling centres and economic-demographic centres of the polities of the time, places where the rulers lived or visited[14]. The residences of the ruler and the highest chiefs would also be expected to become more elaborate. As yet, no archaeological remains of rulers' or high chiefs' houses have been identified anywhere on Oʻahu for this period[15].

A.D. 1400s-1500s
The Unification of the Oʻahu Kingdom
Under ʻEwa (Fig. 2)

...the sea of Ewa, basking in the calm;
The great Ewa (lands) of Laakona
Surrounded by the rain of heaven.
***(The Chant of Kualiʻi.* Fornander 1880:390)**

ORAL ACCOUNTS INDICATE that during the A.D. 1400s,
the island was unified into one polity, which can be called
the Oʻahu Kingdom. Around A.D. 1420-1440, Laʻakona was
the ruler of ʻEwa, Waiʻanae and Waialua Districts, and
evidently he was also recognised as the overall ruler by the
other districts, for in his line 'descended the dignity of Moi
of Oahu' (Fornander 1880:88). Successive rulers came from
this senior Māweke-Kumuhonua line until the reign of
Haka, about A.D. 1520-1540. This senior line held sway
out of royal centres located in ʻEwa, with upland Līhuʻe
near the Waiʻanae Range noted as the major center
(Fornander 1880:88). Virtually nothing is known about this
center, either its *heiau* or residential patterns, or even if it
still has archaeological remains. Also in the uplands of the
ʻEwa polity was an extremely sacred birthing place for the
ruler and chiefs, Kūkaniloko. It had been in use back to the

time of Kapawa in the A.D. 1300s (Kamakau 1991:38).

With island unification, at least three administrative levels of chiefs should have been present—the ruler, high chiefs over one or more districts (or over multiple communities), and local chiefs. It is likely that junior kinsmen of the ruler and high chiefs were appointed over community lands as local chiefs to provision overlords with food, status items, weapons, etc. Most researchers believe that the appointment of such outside chiefs would have replaced local lineage chiefs, led to the breakdown of the local kin groups' corporate control of community lands, and ended commoner kin ties to the ruling chiefs (Hommon 1976, 1986, 1992b:6, Earle 1978:169, Green 1980:73).[16] Some suggest that the resulting land-holding and local political system, termed the *ahupua'a* system, became established in the A.D. 1400s-1500s (Green 1980:75). As yet we have no firm oral historical or archaeological evidence to suggest when the *ahupua'a* system began, and archaeological testing will be difficult (e.g., Green 1980:73; Hommon 1986:65)[17].

About A.D. 1520-1540, Haka assumed the rule of O'ahu and reputedly became 'a stingy, rapacious, and ill-natured chief, who paid no regard to either his chiefs or his commoners' (Kamakau 1991:53-54, Fornander 1880:88). His chiefs slew him at the fortress Waewae near Līhu'e in 'Ewa (Fornander 1880:88). The O'ahu chiefs, 'in council', selected Mā'ilikukahi, from the junior Māweke-Mō'īkeha line, as ruler (Fornander 1880:49, 65, 88). This line controlled the Kona District, so Waikīkī in Kona came to the fore as a royal center (Fornander 1880:89, Kamakau 1991:54). Places in 'Ewa, however, were still periodically used as royal and high chiefly residences (e.g., Piliwale and Lō-Lale living at Līhu'e [Fornander 1880:83, Kamakau 1991:46, 50]), and the Kūkaniloko birthing area remained an important place for all O'ahu high chiefs (Fornander 1880:89, 98).[18] For the remainder of the A.D. 1500s, the rulers are said to have governed over a quiet and prosperous land, all of O'ahu (Fornander 1880:89-91).

Marital links with the rulers and nobility of the Maui and Kaua'i Kingdoms were common at this time (cf. Fornander 1880:84, 87, 89, 91, Kamakau 1991:46, 49, 50). Many chiefly marriages, however, were within the O'ahu Kingdom. These marriages—forging alliances and raising and maintaining ranks—further isolated the highest chiefs and the ruler from the commoners.

The national *heiau* of these centuries would be expected to increase in size, being built or expanded under the ruler's sponsorship. On Maui, *heiau* dating to these years increased in size and invested labour; Pōpōiwi increased to 4727 m² (Kolb 1991:177). Presumably a similar pattern occurred on O'ahu although few large O'ahu *heiau* have been excavated and none dated to this period. Large *heiau* are expected at ruling and *moku* economic-demographic centres—Waikīkī, Honolulu, Kalihi and Moanalua in Kona, throughout the Pearl Harbor lands, Wai'anae, the Waialua-Anahulu area of Waialua, uncertain areas in Ko'olauloa, and the Kāne'ohe Bay, Kailua and Waimānalo areas of Ko'olaupoko.

Lesser *heiau* built by *ahupua'a* level chiefs would also be expected. In Mākaha, the initial phase of Kāne'ākī *heiau*, an open, stepped platform (320 m²), dates to A.D. 1345-1545. Researchers suggested that this was an agricultural *heiau* built by the local chief of Mākaha (Ladd

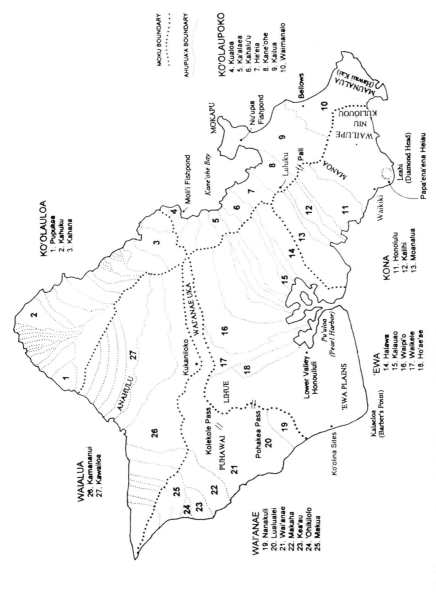

Figure 2: Places mentioned in the later parts of this book.

1973:30, Green 1980:63, 75-76). A walled, 156 m² *heiau* (site 4433) was recently excavated in the mid-areas of Wai'anae Valley, and interpreted as a lesser *heiau*, perhaps agricultural. It is dated to the A.D. 1400s-1600s (Kolb *et al*. n.d.). Pahua *heiau* in Hawai'i Kai is also considered a husbandry *heiau*, and a firepit adjacent to the wall yielded a date in the A.D. 1400s-1600s (Davis 1985:16). This *heiau*, consisting of several connected platforms, had a maximum size of 300 m² and was probably smaller in its earlier form. A lesser *heiau* in Maunawili in Kailua, Kukapoki *heiau*, began as a 300 m² terrace with a date in the A.D. 1300s-1600s; walls were added on at some point after the 1400s (Allen 1989, pers. comm. 1993).

Other larger architectural features which were probably constructed under the sponsorship of the ruler or high chiefs were coastal fishponds[19]. At Honouliuli in 'Ewa, a stone-walled fishpond was built off the shore by the A.D. 1500s (Dicks *et al*. 1987). In Kona, dates from under the fishpond walls of Loko Paweo II in Waikīkī go back to A.D. 1420-1640 (Davis 1989:6). In Ko'olaupoko, the stone-walled Mōli'i fishpond in Kāne'ohe Bay may also date to the A.D. 1400s (Gunness 1993:65). A set of large fishponds (Nu'upia and adjacent ponds) within Kāne'ohe *ahupua'a* appear to have been built during the A.D. 1200s-1600s (Hammatt *et al*. 1985, with the date recalibrated).

Population appears to have been increasing. Permanent houses and agricultural fields had spread in a scattered pattern up the middle and upper portions of Hālawa Valley in 'Ewa (Denison and Foreman 1971, Crozier 1972, Spear 1991) and in Moanalua Valley in Kona (Ayres 1970). In the *ahupua'a* of Waikīkī, a cemetery—a sign of nearby permanent habitation—was at the entrance to Mānoa Valley (Hammatt and Shideler 1991:40). Some subsistence systems were also increasing in size and intensity. Oral histories say that high chief Kalamakua was developing irrigated taro fields on the coastal plain of Waikīkī during the reign of Piliwale, 1560-1580 (cf. Kelly 1989:95, Kamakau 1991:45). In Kailua, the irrigated taro systems were spreading out into Kawainui marsh (Allen-Wheeler 1981). In Kāneʻohe, the wetland terraces (1887) of Luluku were reaching large sizes, as were dryland fields (1888) (Allen *et al.* 1987:230, 241). In Honouliuli in ʻEwa, the irrigated taro fields in the lower valley also seem to have increased in size, with many dates in these centuries (Dicks *et al.* 1987).

In Waiʻanae District, farms and houses were also spreading up into the valleys. Mākaha's dryland fields—informal stone-lined clearings and terraces—spread up the sides of the lower valley in the A.D. 1400s, according to dates from associated field shelters (Green 1980:75). By the A.D. 1500s, the upper valley began to be cultivated in small irrigated taro terraces (Yen *et al.* 1972:89-91). Lualualei's mid-elevations also began to be used, with temporary habitations and associated dryland fields dated to the A.D. 1400s-1600s (Haun 1985:235). In Nānākuli, permanent habitation and dryland fields began to appear in the upper valley at this time (Cordy *et al.* n.d.).

A.D. 1600s-1700s
The Oʻahu Kingdom's
Pinnacle of Power

Kaihikapu-a-Manuia the chief,...Whose temples were thick with kapu.

(Mele koʻihonua of Kalai-kua-hulu. Kamakau 1991:52).

When Ku [Kualiʻi] puts on his girdle of war, you are humbled.

(*The Chant of Kualiʻi*. Fornander 1880:392.)

THE ARCHAEOLOGICAL AND oral historical records indicate that these centuries saw the Oʻahu Kingdom reach its appearance as seen at European contact. The kingdom's ruler held varying degrees of power during these years.

About A.D. 1600-1620, Kalaʻimanuia ruled the entire island. She was born at the Kūkaniloko birthing place, and her main residence was in ʻEwa in Kalauao *ahupuaʻa* (Kamakau 1991:57). Peace prevailed in her time, and she travelled around the island inspecting her lands and rebuilding *heiau* (Kamakau 1991:57). She was particularly noted for having built fishponds, at least three in Kalauao (Fornander 1880:269, Kamakau 1991:57).

About A.D. 1620-1640, dissension arose among her heirs (Fornander 1880:270, Kamakau 1991:60). Kū-a-Manuia ruled out of Waikīkī and controlled the districts of Kona and Koʻolaupoko. His younger brother, Kaʻihikapu-a-Manuia, held lands on the border of Kona and ʻEwa and was in charge of the care of the Mōʻīkeha line's gods Kūkalani and Kūhoʻoneʻenuʻu. The next younger brother, Haʻo, controlled ʻEwa and Waiʻanae; and their sister, Kekela, held Waialua and Koʻolauloa. Kū-a-Manuia—reputedly a poorly-liked ruler—attacked his brother Kaʻihikapu; Haʻo and the populace came to Kaʻihikapu's aid, and Kū was slain (Fornander 1880:270-71, Kamakau 1991:61). Kaʻihikapu became the ruler, moving his base to Waikīkī. Later, Kaʻihikapu grew worried about the size of Haʻo's retinue, after visiting him at Waikele during an official circuit of the island (Fornander 1880:271, Kamakau 1991:64-67). He had Haʻo slain. Haʻo's son, Nāpūlānahumahiki, fled to Waiʻanae, where he formed an independent kingdom. This kingdom also included Waialua and Koʻolauloa, for he married his aunt, Kekela (Fornander 1880:272, Kamakau 1991:67).

This brief split of Oʻahu ended when Kaʻihikapu's son, Kākuhihewa, came to power about A.D. 1640-1660. Kākuhihewa, one of Oʻahu's most renowned rulers, married Kaea-a-Kalona, daughter of Nāpūlānahu and Kekela, reunifying the kingdom (Fornander 1880: 272-73). Kākuhihewa ruled from residences in ʻEwa, Waikīkī and Kailua, with his Kailua residence perhaps most famed in the accounts (Fornander 1880:118-20, 274, 1916-17:274-321, Kamakau 1961:52-55, 1991:69).

Over the next three generations, the ruler gradually lost power to the high chiefs of the districts (Fornander

1880:275-78). The Kona District's high chief and the 'Ewa-Wai'anae high chief seem to have operated fairly independently, with the ruler residing in Ko'olaupoko (Fornander 1880:275-78).

About A.D. 1720-1740, Kuali'i came to power. He re-established the ruler's power by defeating first the Kona chiefs and then the 'Ewa chiefs in battle (Fornander 1880:278-81). Kuali'i also acquired influence over windward Kaua'i, possibly through inheritance (Fornander 1880:277, 288, 293: note 1); and he occasionally visited these Kaua'i lands and placed his junior son, Peleiōholani, over them (Fornander 1880:296). He also initiated war with Ko'olau District on Moloka'i and briefly raided Hilo on Hawai'i (Fornander 1880:281-282). These events mark the expansion of the O'ahu Kingdom outside the island of O'ahu and its rise to power among the islands' kingdoms. These were the first successful expansions of kingdoms to other major islands[20].

Kuali'i's heir, Kapioho'okalani, continued these expansion patterns, leading a force to Moloka'i about A.D. 1740, where he was slain by a Hawai'i army under its ruler, Alapa'inui (Fornander 1880:137-40, Kamakau 1961:70). Alapa'i continued on to O'ahu and landed his force on the windward side. Here, Peleiōholani, brought from Kaua'i as regent for the 6-year old Kanahaokalani, and the O'ahu forces met Alapa'i. A truce was arranged by high chief Na'ili (chief of Wai'anae), as his sister (Kamaka'imoku) had married into the ruling line on Hawai'i and was a wife of Alapa'i and was also the mother of Kalani'ōpu'u and Keōua, the nephews and generals of Alapa'i (Fornander 1880:134-35, Kamakau 1961:71-75). Peleiōholani in later wars conquered

Moloka'i, expanding O'ahu's limits to its largest extent (Fornander 1880:289).

By these centuries, intermarriage among the nobility of all the different kingdoms was occurring with some frequency. The case of Kamaka'imoku, noted above, is one example. Others are the marriage of an O'ahu chieftainess to Kawelo-o-Maihunali'i, ruler of Kaua'i; of a daughter of the Maui ruler to Kuali'i, and of a daughter or a niece of the Kaua'i ruler to Kaho'owahaokalani of O'ahu (Fornander 1880:277, 284, 294). Many other examples exist (cf. Fornander 1880, Kamakau 1961, 1991).

During these centuries, also, increasing administrative complexity of the kingdom is suggested in the oral histories. Before the 1700s, Wai'anae was still apparently administered within 'Ewa. No named high chief, or position, solely over Wai'anae has been found in the author's work with the oral histories. Earlier 'Ewa chiefs controlled Wai'anae. For example, about A.D. 1420-1440, La'akona directly controlled 'Ewa, Wai'anae and Waialua; but he lived in 'Ewa (Fornander 1880:88), and in about 1620-1640 Ha'o, as chief of 'Ewa and Wai'anae, resided in 'Ewa (Fornander 1880:270). This situation changed in the 1700s, when Wai'anae clearly had become a separate administrative unit with a high chief unto itself. About A.D. 1720-1740, Kū a Nu'uanu was the chief of Wai'anae under Kuali'i and his son, Na'ili, followed under Peleiōholani (Fornander 1880:135).

Appointed high chiefs over O'ahu's holdings on Moloka'i and Kaua'i also would have been expected, such as Peleiōholani over Kaua'i. Perhaps such positions were the forerunners of the island 'governor' position often attributed to Kamehameha's time in the 1790s.

High chiefs' residences—a local court with residences of the high chief, local chiefs and hangers-on and associated major *heiau*—were in the prime lands of the kingdom. In the *moku* of Wai'anae, such *heiau* and the high chief's residence were in Wai'anae *ahupua'a* in the Pu'u Kāhea area just back from the shore (Green 1980:6-8). In Waialua, Kamananui was the political center, with *heiau* and chiefly residences (Sahlins 1992: 20-21). In 'Ewa, several high chiefs' courts were present, one being that of Ha'o in Waikele about 1620-1640. Again, the political center of the island was elsewhere, and the district chief and his aides undoubtedly spent time at the ruler's court. The ruling center of Waikīkī would have consisted of the residences of the ruler, high chiefs, low chiefs and hangers-on, as well as residences of the commoners of Waikīkī. Major *heiau* dominated the center; 'Āpuakēhau was on the sand berm and, at contact, Papa'ena'ena *heiau* at the base of Diamond Head overlooked the houses and fields of the Waikīkī plains. An athletic field was adjacent to 'Āpuakēhau (McAllister 1933:77).

The oral accounts indicate that the ruler still travelled around the kingdom, including Moloka'i and parts of Kaua'i in the late 1700s, building or rebuilding major *heiau* and checking on lands, people and the chiefs (e.g., Fornander 1919-20:283). The *heiau* now reached or approached the large size of the rare remaining examples on O'ahu, such as Ulupō (>2006 m²) and Pahukini (1788 m²) in Kailua, Kawa'ewa'e (2820 m²) in Kāne'ohe, and Keaupuni (2323 m²), Punana'ula (966 m²), and Kamohoali'i (892 m²) in Wai'anae (Green 1980:11). On the basis of archaeological evidence, Mākaha's Kāne'ākī *heiau* was rebuilt in the 1700s, becoming a massive structure by the late 1700s (1010 m² by the last stage) (Green 1980:63, 64).

From my reading of the literature, O'ahu's population seems to have been still growing during these centuries. Numerous permanent dwellings were established in Mākaha just below the join of the upper and lower valleys, and a few houses were built in the upper valley (Green 1980:48, 64, 67-68). Lualualei had clusters of permanent housing in its mid and back elevations, beginning in the mid-1600s. Each cluster was 'associated with a heiau and other specialized structures' (Haun 1985:235). Permanent housing also increased in the upper valley of Nānākuli (Cordy *et al.* n.d.), in the mid and upper valleys of Hālawa in 'Ewa (Spear 1991, pers. comm. 1992), and in upland Kāne'ohe (Williams 1992). By contact, it is estimated that O'ahu had at least 43,000-60,000 people within its kingdom, excluding any Kaua'i holdings (Schmitt 1971); possibly the population was higher, between Schmitt's estimates and Stannard's (1989) estimates of >160,000. Missionary censuses from 1835, after a minimum depopulation of about 50%, show O'ahu *ahupua'a* populations commonly in the 200-700 range and some much larger (Schmitt 1973:22-24), so *ahupua'a* populations of 400-1400 may have been quite likely in the 1700s.

By this time, community organization probably no longer saw lineages which held land or which supplied senior members to serve as local chiefs. At contact, local chiefs were appointed by overlord chiefs (Vancouver 1798, I:156, III:66, Menzies 1920:66, 91, and Sahlins' 1992 example of Kualelo appointed on Hawai'i). Land-holding had shifted to a direct relationship between individual households as tenants (*hoa'āina*) and the hierarchy of chiefs who were lords of the land (*haku 'āina*). Commoner households claimed residential and farm land rights as successors of immediate ancestors or affines, and the claims required validation by the local chief (Sahlins 1971, 1973, 1992: cf. 87, 151, 178). Also, commoner marriage became largely endogamous within the *ahupuaʻa* (based on early 1800s marriage records, cf. Sahlins 1992:206-7), possibly as a result of increasing population within communities.

Agricultural fields seem to have undergone some expansion in area. Archaeological work shows agricultural infilling throughout the uppermost reaches of nearly all valleys on Oʻahu by this time: Hālawa Valley in ʻEwa (Spear pers. comm. 1991), Moanalua and Kuliʻouʻou Valleys in Kona (Ayres 1970, Barrera 1979), and Kailua in Koʻolaupoko (Allen pers. comm. 1993). In Waiʻanae, taro pondfields in the upper valley of Mākaha were probably fully expanded in these years, and an irrigation canal and fields were extended down into the lower valley in the 1700s (Green 1980:77-78). The focus of agricultural efforts during these centuries, however, seems to have been on more intensive farming of existing fields.

Settlement, fields and fishponds all probably reached their pre-contact maximum levels in these centuries. Waiʻanae District had dryland farms over considerable portions of the flatlands and gradual slopes, irrigated farms along the springs and streams of Waiʻanae, Mākaha and Pūhāwai in Lualualei, and farms on the central plateau in Waiʻanae uka (Handy and Handy 1972). Fishponds were behind the coastal sand strip, in Mākua, ʻŌhikilolo, Mākaha, Waiʻanae, and Lualualei (Iʻi 1959:23, Green 1980:10, 20, 74, 78, Kelly 1985:251). Houses were scattered. Mākua, ʻŌhikilolo and Keaʻau had a predominantly coastal focus, while Mākaha's housing was both inland and coastal (Green 1980:20-21). The housing of Wai'anae, Lualualei, and Nānākuli had a large coastal focus, but a fair number of houses were in their upper valleys (Haun 1985, Chiu 1992, Denham *et al.* 1992, Cordy *et al.* n.d.).

'Ewa was renowned for its Pearl Harbor irrigated taro lands, and its 36 or so larger fishponds (Kikuchi 1973). The primary taro fields in 'Ewa were on the small floodplains (cf. McDermott 1992), but fields were up the gulches, and dryland farms were on the slopes and upland plateau. Housing was primarily near the shore, yet it extended into the uplands also (witness the royal center at Līhu'e), and some scattered permanent houses were along the shore of the 'Ewa Plain towards Barber's Point. At contact, 'Ewa's population was one of the densest on O'ahu.

In Kona, research into 1840s-1850s land records in Moanalua (Sahlins 1971, 1973), Honolulu (Ono 1992, Kolb *et al.* 1993), Waikīkī (Grune 1993), and Wailupe (Ogata 1992) show shore fishponds (walled-in shallow reefs or modifications of brackish swampy areas behind the sand berms), and often massive taro pondfield systems on coastal plains and lower valley floors, which extended up into the mid and upper valley areas in the large valleys of Nu'uanu and Mānoa. Houses were dense along the shore and were scattered inland, with substantial clusters of inland houses in Waikīkī and Nu'uanu. Drylands were placed into sweet potato, dryland taro, banana, and other cultivation. Archaeological work in Moanalua (Ayres 1970) and Kuli'ou'ou (Barrera 1979) also shows that fields and some scattered houses were all the way up these valleys.

1930 View of Kalokohanahou Fishpond in Kāne'ohe (J. Gilbert McAllister, Bishop Museum photo, Neg. CN 15,361). Such fishponds were built primarily between the 1400s–1700s, when complex societies were present with more powerful rulers and chiefs. These chiefs were able to call together large groups of people for public works projects.

Oral historical and early archaeological work (e.g., Thrum 1907, McAllister 1933) show large *heiau* in many communities, with the extremely important national *heiau* of Papaʻenaʻena and ʻĀpuakēhau in Waikīkī.

In Koʻolaupoko, Kailua and Kāneʻohe Bay were the economic and demographic centres of the *moku*. At Kailua, Māhele land records (Cordy 1977a, Kelly and Nakamura 1981, Creed 1992) show houselots along the sand shore berm and in large numbers on the slopes around the lower valley marshes (Kawainui and Kaʻelepulu), particularly at the entrance of upper valley streams. The ruler's residence had been on the beach berm. Large *heiau* were present around Kawainui Marsh (Ulupō, Pahukini). Taro cultivation was in extensive pondfields on the infilling fringes of the marsh at the deltas of the streams, with archaeological work suggesting expansion into the marsh continuing in the 1700s (Cordy 1977b). As well, the pondfields extended all the way back up the upper valleys' floors as descending terraces. Dry fields of sweet potatoes, bananas, and taro were on the slopes fringing the marsh and upper valleys. The marsh also included a large inland fishpond. In contrast, work with Māhele records in the Kāneʻohe Bay area (Devaney *et al.* 1976, Cordy 1977c, Nettles 1992) indicates that most of the housing was focused along the bay in drier areas along the lower valleys. Housing was also scattered in small clusters in the upper valleys. Large *heiau* were on the tips of ridges or hillsides (McAllister 1933:168, 173, 177, 179). Irrigated taro fields covered narrow valley floors (Kāneʻohe), wide valley floors (Kaʻalaea and Kahaluʻu), lower valley marshes (Heʻeia), and extended up nearly all tributary streams to the base of the *pali* with the Luluku system in

Kāne'ohe being among the largest. At least 23 stone-walled fishponds were built out into the bay's shallow waters.

In central Waialua, similarly, the lower valley and coastal plains were extensively modified into irrigated pondfields with some sizeable inland fishponds (e.g., 'Uko'a) built along the major streams (Sahlins 1992). Large *heiau* were near the shore in Kamananui (Sahlins 1992:20-21), and residences were scattered across the dry areas along with dryland fields. The narrower upper valley had irrigated pondfields on each stream flat along with temporary residences and dry field areas. Archaeological work in upper Anahulu Valley shows that permanent habitations spread there only in the late 1700s or early 1800s (Kirch and Spriggs 1993:6-7). Archival work suggests this spread occurred in the early 1800s and was caused by the settling-in of Kamehameha's Hawai'i followers and by the high chiefs' and ruler's demands for more supplies (Sahlins 1992).

Major trails linked O'ahu's communities and had probably been present for centuries. One path ran around the island along the shore. A major side branch cut inland across the 'Ewa Plain, by-passing the sparsely populated shore of the 'Ewa Plain (I'i 1959:97). Major trails crossed the central plateau, tying Waialua's communities to those of 'Ewa. Two trails branched off and crossed the Wai'anae mountains, connecting Wai'anae to 'Ewa (I'i 1959:97). Other trails crossed the Ko'olaus, the most noted being the Pali trail from Nu'uanu in Kona which descended with branches into Kailua, Waimānalo and Kāne'ohe in Ko'olaupoko.

1836 View of the Cross-Island Trail over the Pali between Nuʻuanu and Kailua (Vaillant expedition, Photo from Hawaiʻi State Archives, Neg. 17,038). The Pali trail was one of the main cross-island trails of the Oʻahu Kingdom from the A.D. 1400s–1700s. It may well have been an even older trail connecting different countries of earlier times.

1780s and 1790s

O'ahu Conquered
by the Maui Kingdom and then
by the Hawai'i Kingdom

I am looking around, desiring the sight [of my chief].
I do not see him, he has forever disappeared.

(Kalawela, *A Lamentation for Kahahana*.
Fornander 1919-20:296.)

WITH THE DEATH of Peleiōholani about 1779, O'ahu's Kingdom began a rapid collapse, being outcompeted by the Maui Kingdom within the growing arena of interisland conquest. Peleiōholani's son, Kumuhana, proved to be incompetent and was removed, departing for his family's lands in Kaua'i, where his son Kāneoneo had risen to power by marrying Kaua'i's ruler Kamakahelei (Fornander 1880:291, Beaglehole 1967:3). Kahahana was selected as ruler. He was the son of a powerful 'Ewa high chief ('Elani), and his mother was a sister of Peleiōholani (Fornander 1919-20:282). Kahahana, however, had been raised at Kahekili's court on Maui, as his mother was also related to Kahekili and the Maui royal line (Fornander 1919-20:282). And so enters Kahekili into the picture, one of the most able and powerful rulers in the islands at European contact and just after.

Kahekili quickly subverted Kahahana's rule, and duped him into capturing his own high priest and wisest advisor, Kaʻopulupulu, in Waiʻanae where Kahahana was refurbishing Kamohoaliʻi *heiau*. Kaʻopulupulu was slain and offered up on the *heiau* in Waikīkī. With the high priest dead, a Maui army invaded and conquered the Oʻahu Kingdom about 1783 (Fornander 1880:225, Kamakau 1961:132-36). After hiding in he mountains for two years, Kahahana was captured and slain in 1785. His remains were probably offered up to the Maui Kingdom's gods at Papaʻenaʻena *heiau* on the slopes of Diamond Head. The slaying of Kahahana led to a revolt by Oʻahu's chiefs with ʻElani, his father, as a leader along with a few Maui and Kauaʻi chiefs (most notably Kāneoneo, Peleiōholani's grandson)(Fornander 1880:225-27, 1919- 20:290-91, Kamakau 1961: 138-40). The rebels' success seems to have been limited to the slaying of Hueu, the Maui high chief in control of Waialua District (Kamakau 1961:138). The revolt was brutally crushed and Kāneoneo slain (Kamakau 1961:138-40, Barrère 1970:52-54).

Fearfully did Kahekili avenge the death of Hueu on the revolted Oʻahu chiefs. Gathering his forces together, he overran the districts of Kona and ʻEwa, and a war of extermination ensued. Men, women, and children were killed without discrimination and without mercy. The streams of Makaho and Niuhelewai in Kona, and that of Hoaiai [Hoʻeʻae] in ʻEwa, are said to have been literally choked with the corpses of the slain. The native Oʻahu aristocracy were almost entirely extirpated (Fornander 1880:226).

Many of the Maui chiefs then settled down on the abundant, well-watered wet taro lands of O'ahu. Indeed, Kahekili primarily used Waikīkī as his royal center up to his death in 1794.

In 1794, after Kahekili's death, his half-brother, Kā'eo Kulani, ruler of Kaua'i and ally to Maui, was returning home from the wars against Kamehameha. Kahekili's son and heir, Kalanikūpule, was on O'ahu. Suspicions arose between the Kaua'i and Maui camps, and a series of battles were fought on O'ahu (Fornander 1880:262-65, Kamakau 1961: 168-69). This event might be interpreted as a rare and little noted attempt of the Kaua'i Kingdom to expand against the Maui Kingdom. Ka'eo was aided by Waialua's and Wai'anae's warriors. Ka'eo won the first three battles in 'Ewa, but in a final battle in 'Ewa, he and many of his chiefs were slain, ending Kaua'i's brief fling at interisland conquest.

In 1795, after little more than a decade of control on O'ahu, the Maui Kingdom's forces were beaten in battle at Nu'uanu by the forces of Kamehameha's Hawai'i Kingdom. O'ahu lands were now parcelled out to the high chiefs and lesser chiefs of the Hawai'i Kingdom (cf. Sahlins 1992; Kame'eleihiwa 1986), and many of the *heiau* were rededicated to Hawai'i Kingdom gods. After two failed attempts to reach and conquer Kaua'i in 1796 and 1803-1804, Kamehameha, like Kahekili, remained on O'ahu with his residence first at Waikīkī and then at Honolulu. His high chiefs, lesser chiefs and many warriors and their families also settled down on O'ahu. This affected settlement (Sahlins 1992:39-40, 52-53), but this is a story of the Hawai'i Kingdom, and no longer that of the O'ahu Kingdom.

Discussion

WHAT KINDS OF new perspectives result from an island overview such as this one? Compared with the overly general archipelago scenarios, the island view allows a more focused look at environmental variations, subsistence development, population changes, political and social organization, and stimulates thoughts on interrelations. Such an overview also enables a better perspective of political histories and dynamics among the polities, raising district studies into a wider context. Linkage of archaeology with social anthropological evidence from oral histories also comes more easily at this level, for in late prehistory (A.D. 1300s onwards), the oral accounts focus on polities (and their rulers) and relations between them.

For example, the oral histories suggest complex societies emerged on Oʻahu no later than the early A.D. 1300s in three main centres: ʻEwa, Kona and Koʻolaupoko. ʻEwa then unified the island in the 1400s. For those interested in the early formation of complex societies and associated changes in population, subsistence systems and religious structures, this information suggests that perhaps more attention should be directed toward the ʻEwa area. Later, Waikīkī in Kona became the primary royal center, with Kailua and some 'Ewa areas occasionally also used as royal centres. Perhaps study of changes in population, subsistence and religious structures in such political centres compared with the outlying districts could produce interesting results. It should not be forgotten that Moloka'i and part of Kaua'i were outlying areas within the O'ahu Kingdom in the 1700s before its conquest.

Another point relates to population growth. Permanent habitation seems to have been restricted to windward lands up into the A.D. 900s, with agricultural expansion into the upper windward valleys occurring much earlier than previously thought. Between the A.D. 1000s and 1300s, population still seems to have been increasing in windward lands, and a rapid expansion into the leeward side's lower valleys seems to have occurred. Another rapid spurt of population may have occurred island-wide in the 1400s-1500s. These points suggest rapid and differential population growth (windward *versus* leeward), rather than the gradual curves which we have produced with a single boom in the A.D. 1400s-1600s. Perhaps we should begin to consider the possibility of multiple rapid spurts and how they may relate to changes in subsistence and political organization.

Also, the overview shows that there are some notable differences between this island and the drier islands of Hawai'i and Maui. O'ahu has far greater stream and valley development, particularly on leeward sides. The greatest percentages of each community's agricultural lands on O'ahu were generally on coastal plains and in lower valleys. Upper valley agricultural fields generally covered smaller areas and were not large inland systems. This contrasts with leeward Hawai'i and Maui where perennial streams were generally lacking and where the primary fields were situated on the upland slopes at elevations where rainfall enabled reliable dryland cultivation. Thus, the idea of inland expansion being a major factor in the establishment of self-sufficient communities and community organization changes, while perhaps feasible for leeward Hawai'i and Maui, seems less applicable in the O'ahu case.

Last, there are signs of increasing permanent habitations and agricultural expansion right up to contact, despite archipelago models of population levelling or declining. This suggests population and agricultural expansion and intensification threshholds had not yet been reached—a point long held by a number of us and made strikingly clear by the immediate post-contact upper valley agricultural intensification and population expansion in Anahulu. Kamehameha was also said to have expanded irrigated taro lands in Waikīkī and Nu'uanu (cf. Sahlins 1992:52), so Anahulu may not be a rarity. This question of population and agricultural growth in late prehistory needs more research. Fascinating data on population and agricultural change are now being presented using plots of charcoal dates (e.g., Allen 1992, Dye and Komori 1992, Williams 1992), but bits of information in this overview lead to a question as to whether the late prehistoric charcoal date declines are accurate reflections of population and agricultural growth. Agricultural charcoal decline may be caused by intensification of agriculture with fewer fallow periods and less charcoal left from clearing and burning (cf. Dye and Komori 1992, Hommon 1992a:8). Habitation charcoal declines could be a result of problems with the data base (cf. Dye and Komori 1992 for a discussion of some possible problems.) I would suggest archaeologists tend to date earlier samples from their sites, thus underrepresenting dates at the end of prehistory. If the data base concerns can be addressed, and if a focus on islands and districts can occur, then fascinating pictures of population and agricultural dynamics could result. Also, more specific settlement archaeology case studies such as Mākaha could evaluate whether agriculture and population were still growing at the end of prehistory.

1857 View of Coastal Housing in the Honolulu to Waikīkī Area (G.H. Burgess lithograph, Photo from Hawai'i State Archives, Neg. 16,576). Waikīkī and Honolulu both had vast areas of irrigated kalo and sizable populations. This view shows dense coastal housing and associated coconuts and other trees. Waikīkī had been a royal center since the mid-1500s, the time of Mā'ilikūkahi.

Notes

1. Kahoʻolawe—a small island, but not a traditional district—is equivalent to the district level of analysis (cf. Hommon 1980, Rosendahl *et al.* 1987). The same could be said of any future studies of Lānaʻi or Niʻihau.

2. Kolb (1991, 1994) conducted an island study of Maui which focuses on *heiau* and political change.

3. Based on Stearns and Vaksvik 1935, Stearns 1966, Carlquist 1970, Macdonald and Abbott 1970, Beggerly 1990, Cuddihy and Stone 1990.

4. Researchers a few years ago argued that the Bellows coastal plain was a marine bay or estuary prior to A.D. 1000 (Athens 1988, Beggerly 1990); recent work indicates that this was not the case (Shun 1992).

5. Specific radiocarbon dates are presented using the calibrated ages as published by the authors.

6. These dates show inland agricultural expansion before the A.D. 1400s, contradicting the 'inland expansion' model initially offered by Hommon (1976). If the model is altered for inland expansion 100-200 years earlier in windward areas (cf. Hommon 1976:274, 1992b:5, Allen *et al.* 1987:249-50), these dates are still too early. New thought should be given to the concept of inland expansion, because variations in population growth probably occurred. Early windward communities probably had earlier population growth and earlier expansion of farms inland. Kāneʻohe, with narrow valley floodplains near the shore, may have expanded inland earlier than most windward communities. On leeward sides, some areas may have expanded inland about A.D. 1400; others may have expanded much later. The concept of expanding inland within community lands is a sound one, as is the concept of increased inland use. Attempting to use too arbitrary a date (post-A.D. 1400) may have disadvantages.

7. For a listing, see Hunt and Holden (1991) or Spriggs and Anderson (1993). Spriggs and Anderson reject many early dates, often for being solitary or

much older dates in a set of more recent ones. These dates, however, could be accurate, with later dates being evidence of lateral spread and deepening of deposits. Cautions about older dates—particularly in relation to the problem of old wood (Dye pers. comm. 1993)—are needed, but over-caution and the resulting discard of many dates may have hazards too.

8. Handy considered the Koʻolaupoko-Koʻolauloa border area an early centre of colonisation because of the many oral traditions about early figures in Hawaiian mythology: where Wākea and Haumea lived, where their son Hāloa (associated with taro) was born, where Wākea battled with Kumuhonua, where Kamapuaʻa was born and lived in his youth, etc. (Handy and Handy 1972:436-37). These accounts may well be evidence of early settlement and bear further study.

9. Perhaps the inclusion of Maunalua (Hawaiʻi Kai) as an *'ili* of Waimānalo— a part of Koʻolaupoko—at European contact is a remnant pattern of earlier land claims of windward populations.

10. Genealogy based on Kamakau (1991:77-79, 1961:66-75, 128-41, 1964:note 4, p.23), Malo (n.d.) and Fornander (1878:89, 196, App.IX:lines 29-53, 1880:48-49, 68, 86-91, 269-91). [Fornander incorrectly has Kaʻihikapu-a -Kākuhihewa as father of Kahoʻowaha in Appendix IX (1878) but his text correctly identifies Kānekapu-a -Kākuhihewa as the father (1880:277-78). Cf. Barrère 1991:87-8, note 33, for same conclusion.] Fornander and Kamakau agree, except that Fornander inserts an extra generation prior to Māʻilikūkahi, with Kūkahiʻililani as the father (1878:App. IX, 1919, 6(2):313), while Kamakau (1991:53) has Puaʻa-a-Kahuoi as Māʻilikūkahi's father. [Malo skips three generations from Kapae a Laʻakona to Haka.] This genealogy agrees with Hommon (1976), with the exception that Hommon has Haka one generation earlier and not of the same generation as Māʻilikūkahi. Laʻakona is also called Lakona (Fornander 1878:88), ʻEwa-uli-a-Laʻakona and ʻEwa-nui-a-Laʻakona (Kamakau 1991:36, Fornander 1880:90, Barrère 1991:85 note 21). Peleiōholani lived to an old age, with his reign spanning the time when the next generation came of age. Yet the dates for the next generation are consistent. For example, Kanahaokalani was a child *ca.* A.D. 1740.

11. Oral histories on Hawaiʻi Island show some polities there of similar hierarchical organisation were smaller than traditional districts (Cordy 1994). For example, Northern Kohala was divided into two polities, Kukuipahu and Niuliʻi (cf. Fornander 1918-19:215-20).

12. Some argue that human sacrifice and Kū worship became dominant on Hawaiʻi Island and Maui, beginning with Pāʻao and Pili in the A.D. 1400s, while the Oʻahu national religion did not have human sacrifice or Kū as a dominant factor until the Maui conquest in 1783. Kamakau (1991:56) states, 'It is said of Maʻilikukahi that he did not sacrifice men in the *heiau*

and *luakini*. That was the way of the Kukaniloko chiefs. There were no sacrificial *heiau, po'o kanaka*, there.' Some cautions need to be given. One, the main national gods of the O'ahu rulers 'from remote times to the times of 'Kahahana' included Kūho'ohe'enu'u and Kūkalani (Kamakau 1991:8). They are specifically noted in the reign of Kū-a-manuia, 1620-1640 (Fornander 1880:270, Kamakau 1991:60). Both were Kū forms and were associated with human sacrifice at contact (Kamakau 1964:12, 1976:140) and presumably earlier, since one of Kamakau's main instructors was his *kapunakane* (grandfather or granduncle) who was evidently a priest under the O'ahu or Kaua'i Kingdom. Two, a fair number of *po'o kanaka heiau* on O'ahu were identified by informants in the late 1800s and early 1900s (cf. Thrum 1907:44-48, McAllister 1933). Three, Kolb's (1991) work on Maui shows that dog, pig and human bone do not start appearing in the refuse on large national *heiau* until the 1600s-1700s. Perhaps this was true across the islands, even on Hawai'i. Perhaps a shift to greater human sacrifices occurred at this time on O'ahu also, which would be compatible with the national gods of O'ahu being Kū gods associated with human sacrifice and would also be compatible with the numerous large sacrificial *heiau*. Undoubtedly, there were differences in the religions of the kingdoms (seen, for example, in image form), and there are clues that O'ahu's religion may have been somewhat different. But this needs careful study.

13. Kolb (pers. comm. 1993) cautions that national *heiau* may not have been much larger than other *heiau* at this time.

14. At European contact, a few large *heiau* were also found in areas not normally associated with prior political-economic centres. In some cases, they were built for a specific event (e.g., the seizure and sacrifice of a rebel chief).

15. Chiefly residences were identified in Hālawa (Crozier 1972), but the evidence for these sites being chiefly is minimal. It is to be hoped it will be reanalysed in the Bishop Museum's forthcoming highway studies of Hālawa *ahupua'a*.

16. Thought needs to be given to the process of supplanting local lineage chiefs. Under island unification, if peaceably attained, local lineage chiefs could have been left in place. Or, only areas outside 'Ewa may have had new local chiefs appointed, and a mixed system would result. In Pohnpei in Micronesia, appointed local chiefs married into local lineages and their heirs as local chiefs were often part of the local lineage system (Riesenberg 1968). Sahlins' work in Waialua also shows marriage between more important commoners and lesser local chiefs (1992:208, 211).

17. Archaeologists have suggested that massive inland agricultural expansion and population growth about A.D. 1400-1500 led to community self-sufficiency and then to the disintegration of the lineages and to the formation of *ahupua'a* (cf. Hommon 1976, 1986). However, earlier O'ahu

communities should have been self-sufficient in daily subsistence, as they farmed lower valleys and coastal plains, had adjacent fisheries, and had inland forest sources just as did later *ahupua'a*. On O'ahu, most farmlands and the bulk of the population remained focused nearer the sea throughout prehistory (with exceptions). The key change seems to be the appointment of outside chiefs as managers to extract resources for overlord chiefs (cf. Hommon 1992b:6) and the eventual end of lineage chiefs and lineage land control. As yet, we have not identified the start of this outside lord to local tenant change archaeologically. Oral histories might provide clues. Mā'ilikūkahi, 1520-1540, is credited with resolving the confusion over *ahupua'a* borders, with clearly demarcating them, and with assigning chiefs to the *ahupua'a* (Kamakau 1991:54-55). This has been argued by some to mark the start of the *ahupua'a* land unit. But, did Mā'ilikūkahi create a new system or did he alter existing community borders? Perhaps the fact that a ruler could change borders implies some outside control, but whether the assigned chiefs were local lineage chiefs or outsider appointees is uncertain. Oral histories from Hawai'i referring to 'Umi's reign, A.D. 1600-1620, describe a similar situation with his two high priests altering the borders of existing community land units in Ka'ū District (Boundary Commission Books 1870s-1880s, Hawaii, A:404, 439). The oral records could perhaps be searched to identify appointments of outside chiefs over single *ahupua'a*. For example, Līloa seems to have appointed his son's ('Umi's) commoner mother as a local chief over a community about 1580-1600 (Kamakau 1961:8). Also, the oral records could be carefully checked for the appearance of elements of the tenant-lord relation: seasonal tribute (the *ho'okupu* of the *makahiki*), corvee labour, requisitions of food and other items demanded by the lord (Sahlins 1992:cf. 87). As one example, *koele* fields (corvee labour taro fields) were said to be created by Kīla under the Waipi'o ruler Kunaka in the late 1300s (Fornander 1916-17:134-36).

18. The rulers from Mā'ilikūkahi through Kūkaniloko also had ties to 'Ewa, for they were 'Lō' chiefs whose historical home was the uplands of Līhu'e and adjacent Wahiawa and Halemano (Kamakau 1964:5, 1991:40).

19. Caution should be given to the assumption that all fishpond construction was initiated by the ruler and high chiefs. Kāne'ohe *ahupua'a* had an average of almost one fishpond per *'ili* (subdivisions of an *ahupua'a*). 'Ili level construction by local chiefs and commoners may have been initiated for subsistence purposes. Many smaller fishponds were also constructed by commoners within the irrigated taro fields of the lower valley.

20. Maui, under Kamalālāwalu, tried to invade the Hawai'i Kingdom about A.D. 1640-1660, but he was defeated by the armies of the reinstated Lonoikamakahiki and slain. Kalani'ōpu'u of Hawai'i successfully expanded his kingdom's borders to include the Hana and Kipahulu areas of Maui about 1760-1780, not long after O'ahu's expansion.

References

(Parentheses with O-and H-numbers at the end of citations refer to the library numbers in the State Historic Preservation Division library.)

Allen, J., 1989. Preliminary Report: Archaeological Investigations at Sites 50-Oa-G6-17 and G6-69 through G6-71, Royal Hawaiian Country Club Inc., Makai Golf Course Project Area, Maunawili, Kailua, Koʻolaupoko, Oʻahu. Manuscript, Department of Anthropology, Bernice P. Bishop Museum, Honolulu (O-840).

—— 1992. Farming in Hawaiʻi from colonisation to contact: Radiocarbon chronology and implications for cultural change. *New Zealand Journal of Archaeology*, 14:45-66.

Allen, J., M. Riford, T. Bennett, G. Murakami and M. Kelly, 1987. Five Upland ʻIli: Archaeological and Historical Investigations in the Kāneʻohe Interchange, Interstate Highway H-3, Island of Oʻahu. Report 87-1. Department of Anthropology, Bernice P. Bishop Museum, Honolulu.

Allen-Wheeler, J., 1981. Archaeological Excavations in Kawainui Marsh, Island of Oʻahu. Manuscript, Department of Anthropology, Bernice P. Bishop Museum, Honolulu.

Athens, J.S., 1988. Archaeological Survey and Testing for Airfield Perimeter Fence Project, Bellows Air Force Station, Oahu, Hawaii. Manuscript, International Archaeological Research Institute Inc., Honolulu (O-431).

Athens, J.S. and J. Ward, 1991. Paleoenvironmental and Archaeological Investigations, Kawainui Marsh Flood Control Project, Oʻahu Island, Hawaiʻi. Manuscript, International Archaeological Research Institute Inc., Honolulu (O-719).

Ayres, W., 1970. Archaeological Survey and Excavations, Kamana-Nui Valley, Moanalua Ahupuaʻa, South Halawa Valley, Halawa Ahupuaʻa. Report 70-8. Department of Anthropology, Bernice P. Bishop Museum, Honolulu.

Barrera, W., 1979. Kuliʻouʻou Valley Excavations. Manuscript, Chiniago Inc., Honolulu (0-77).

Barrère, D., 1970. An historical sketch of Makaha Valley. In R.C. Green (ed.), *Makaha Valley Historical Project: Interim Report 2*. Pacific Anthropological Records 10:3-14. Honolulu, Department of Anthropology, Bernice P. Bishop Museum.

—— 1991. Notes. In S. Kamakau, *Tales and Traditions of the People of Old: Na Moʻolelo a ka Poʻe Kahiko*. Honolulu, Bishop Museum Press.

Bath, J., M. Rosendahl and P. Rosendahl, 1984. Subsurface Archaeological Reconnaissance Survey: Kuilima Resort Expansion Project. Manuscript, PHRI, Hilo.

Beaglehole, J.C. (ed.), 1967. *The Journals of Captain James Cook on his Voyages of Discovery. III. The Voyage of the Resolution and Discovery, 1776-1780*. Cambridge, Hakluyt Society.

Beggerly, P., 1990. Kahana Valley, Hawaiʻi, a Geomorphic Artifact: A Study of the Interrelationships among Geomorphic Structures, Natural Processes, and Ancient Hawaiian Technology, Land Use and Settlement Patterns. Unpublished Ph.D. dissertation, University of Hawaii at Manoa.

Boundary Commission Books, 1870s-1880s. *Boundary Commission Books*. 5 vols. Microfilm, Archives of the State of Hawaii, Honolulu.

Burtchard, G., 1992. Historic Preservation Mitigation Plan, Development Parcel 34, Keauhou, North Kona, Island of Hawaiʻi. Manuscript, International Archaeological Research Institute Inc., Honolulu.

Carlquist, S., 1970. *Hawaii, A Natural History*. Garden City, The Natural History Press.

Cartwright, B., 1930. Note on Hawaiian genealogies. *38th Annual Report of the Hawaiian Historical Society for the Year 1929*, pp.45-47. Honolulu.

Charvet-Pond, A. and B. Davis, 1991. Draft: Volume I: West Beach Data Recovery Program. Phase 4 — Archaeological and Paleontological Excavations. Ko Olina Resort, Land of Honouliuli, ʻEwa, Island of Oahu. Manuscript, PHRI, Hilo (O-869).

Chiu, M-Y., 1992. Waiʻanae Ahupuaʻa: An Overview of Historic Preservation (Archaeological Sites). Manuscript, State Historic Preservation Division, Honolulu.

Clark, J.T., 1980. Phase I — Archaeological Survey of Castle Estate Lands Around the Kawainui Marsh, Kailua, Oʻahu. Manuscript, Department of Anthropology, Bernice P. Bishop Museum, Honolulu (O-96).

Cordy, R., 1974a. Cultural adaptation and evolution in Hawaii: A suggested new sequence. *Journal of the Polynesian Society*, 83:180-91.

—— 1974b. Complex rank cultural systems in the Hawaiian Islands: Suggested explanations for their origin. *Archaeology and Physical Anthropology in Oceania*, 9:89-109.

—— 1977a. *A Cultural Resources Study for the City and County of Honolulu's Permit Request: Kawainui Marsh Sewerline (Oahu). Archaeological Reconnaissance and Pre-1850 Literature Search*. Honolulu, U.S. Army Corps of Engineers.

—— 1977b. Site 7, Kawainui Marsh (Kailua Ahupuaʻa, Oahu Island): Test Excavations. Manuscript, U.S. Army Corps of Engineers, Fort Shafter, Honolulu (O-198).

—— 1977c. Kaneohe Bay Urban Water Resources Study, Cultural Resources Study: Cultural Resources Planning. Manuscript, U.S. Army Corps of Engineers, Fort Shafter, Honolulu.

—— 1978. A Study of Prehistoric Social Change: The Development of Complex Societies in the Hawaiian Islands. Unpublished Ph.D. dissertation, University of Hawaii at Manoa.

—— 1981. *A Study of Prehistoric Social Change: The Development of Complex Societies in the Hawaiian Islands*. New York, Academic Press.

—— 1985. Settlement patterns of complex societies in the Pacific. *New Zealand Journal of Archaeology*, 7:159-82.

—— 1987a. Hamakua and Waipiʻo: The Homeland of Hawaiʻi Island's Political System. Manuscript, State Historic Preservation Division, Honolulu.

—— 1987b. An Overview of Kaʻu District and Some Thoughts on Island-Wide Settlement Patterns. Paper presented at the 1st Annual Society for Hawaiian Archaeology Conference, Hawaii Volcanoes National Park. Manuscript, State Historic Preservation Division, Honolulu.

—— 1992. Ideas from the Oral Historical Record: Formative Complex Societies — The Prelude to Island Unification. Paper presented at 5th Annual Society for Hawaiian Archaeology Conference, Kauaʻi.

—— 1994. A Regional Synthesis of Hāmākua District, Hawaiʻi Island. Manuscript, State Historic Preservation Division, Honolulu.

Cordy, R., N. Pak, C. Johnson, M.J. Lee and M. McFadden, n.d. Nānākuli: A Leeward Oʻahu Valley. Draft manuscript, State Historic Preservation Division, Honolulu.

Cordy, R. and H.D. Tuggle, 1976. Bellows, Oahu, Hawaiian Islands: New work and new interpretations. *Archaeology and Physical Anthropology in Oceania*, 11:207-35.

Creed, V., 1992. Settlement Pattern for Kailua Ahupuaʻa, Koʻolaupoko, Oʻahu. Manuscript, State Historic Preservation Division, Honolulu.

Crozier, S.N., 1972. A Preliminary Report on the Phase II, Part 2 Survey of H-3 Highway Corridor in the South Halawa Valley, Oahu. Manuscript, Department of Anthropology, Bernice P. Bishop Museum, Honolulu (O-51).

Cuddihy, L. and C. Stone, 1990. *Alteration of Native Hawaiian Vegetation: Effects of Humans, Their Activities and Introductions*. Honolulu, University of Hawaii Cooperative National Park Resources Studies Unit.

Davis, B., 1985. A Report on the Stabilization and Partial Restoration of Pahua Heiau, Maunalua (Hawaii Kai), Oahu. Manuscript, Department of Anthropology, Bernice P. Bishop Museum, Honolulu (O-315).

—— 1989. Subsurface Archaeological Reconnaissance Survey and Historical Research at Fort DeRussy, Waikiki, Island of Oʻahu, Hawaiʻi. Manuscript, International Archaeological Research Institute Inc., Honolulu (O-607).

—— 1990. Archaeological Assessment of Proposed Developments at the U.S. Naval Base, Pearl Harbor, Oʻahu, Hawaiʻi. Manuscript, International Archaeological Research Institute Inc., Honolulu (O-655).

—— 1991. Archaeological Monitoring of Environmental Baseline Survey and Excavations in Hawaiian Land Commission Award 1515 ('Apana 2) at Fort DeRussy, Waikiki, Oʻahu. Manuscript, International Archaeological Research Institute Inc., Honolulu (O-834).

Davis, B. and A. Haun, 1986. Preliminary Report upon Completion of Field Work: Phase 2, Intensive Survey and Test Excavations, West Beach Data Recovery Program. Manuscript, PHRI, Hilo.

Davis, B., A. Haun and P. Rosendahl, 1986. Phase 3 — Data Recovery Plan for Archaeological and Paleontological Excavations, West Beach Data Recovery Program. Manuscript, PHRI, Hilo (O-587).

Davis, B. and M. Kaschko, 1980. Use and Abandonment of Habitation Caves in the Prehistoric Settlement of Southeastern Oahu: A Proposed Research Design for the 1980 University of Hawaii Archaeological Field Program. Manuscript, University of Hawaii, Honolulu (O-184).

Denham, T., P. Brennan, J. Ward and S. Avery, 1993. Draft: Paleoenvironmental Reconstruction Adjacent to the Mouth of Halawa Stream: Monitoring Report of the Waiau-Makalapa No. 2 138 kV Overhead Lines (Phase II), Halawa Ahupuaʻa, ʻEwa District, Island of Oʻahu. Manuscript, Archaeological Consultants of Hawaii, Pupukea (O-808).

Denham, T., J. Kennedy and L. Reintsema, 1992. Archaeological Inventory Survey with Subsurface Testing Report for a Property Located at TMK: 8-5-02:48, Waianae Ahupuaʻa. Manuscript, Archaeological Consultants Hawaii, Pupukea.

Denison, D. and A. Foreman, 1971. 1971 Archaeological Investigations in South Halawa Valley, ʻEwa District, Island of Oahu — Phase II. Report 71-9. Department of Anthropology, Bernice P. Bishop Museum, Honolulu (O-45).

Devaney, D., M. Kelly, P.J. Lee and L.S. Motteler, 1976. *Kaneʻohe: A History of Change (1778-1950)*. Honolulu, Bernice P. Bishop Museum.

Dicks, M., A. Haun and P. Rosendahl, 1987. Archaeological Reconnaissance Survey for Environmental Impact Statement: West Loch Estates — Golf Course and Parks, Land of Honouliuli, Ewa District, Island of Oahu. Manuscript, PHRI, Hilo (O-437).

Dunn, A., A. Haun and S. Goodfellow, 1991. Intensive Archaeological Survey and Test Excavations, 'Ewa Marina Community Project — Phase I. Manuscript, PHRI, Hilo (O-675).

Dye, T., 1977. Archaeological Phase I Survey of the Leeward Portion of Proposed Interstate H-3, North Halawa, Oahu. Manuscript, Department of Anthropology, Bernice P. Bishop Museum, Honolulu (O-130).

—— 1989. Tales of two cultures: Traditional historical and archaeological interpretations of Hawaiian prehistory. *Bishop Museum Occasional Papers*, 29:3-22. Honolulu.

—— 1992. The South Point radiocarbon dates thirty years later. *New Zealand Journal of Archaeology*, 14:89-97.

Dye, T. and E. Komori, 1992. A pre-censal population history of Hawai'i. *New Zealand Journal of Archaeology*, 14:113-28.

Dye, T. and D. Steadman, 1990. Polynesian ancestors and their animal world. *American Scientist*, 78:207-15.

Earle, T., 1973. Control Hierarchies in the Traditional Irrigation Economy of Halele'a District, Kaua'i, Hawaii. Unpublished Ph.D. dissertation, University of Michigan, Ann Arbor.

—— 1978. *Economic and Social Organization of a Complex Chiefdom: The Halele'a District, Kaua'i, Hawaii*. Anthropological Papers of the Museum of Anthropology, University of Michigan 63. Ann Arbor.

Emory, K.P. and Y.H. Sinoto, 1961. *Hawaiian Archaeology: Oahu Excavations*. Bernice P. Bishop Museum Special Publication 49. Honolulu, Bishop Museum Press.

Erkelens, C., 1993. The Archaeological Investigation of the Kukanono Slope, Kawainui Marsh, Kailua, Ko'olaupoko, O'ahu. Unpublished M.A. thesis, Department of Anthropology, University of Hawaii at Manoa.

Fornander, A., 1878. *An Account of the Polynesian Race. Its Origin and Migrations and the Ancient History of the Hawaiian People to the Times of Kamehameha I*. Volume I. London, Trübner.

—— 1880. *An Account of the Polynesian Race. Its Origin and Migrations and the Ancient History of the Hawaiian People to the Times of Kamehameha I*. Volume II. London, Trübner.

—— 1916-17, 1918-19, 1919-20. *Fornander Collection of Hawaiian Antiquities and Folk-lore*. Memoirs of the Bernice P. Bishop Museum 4, 5 and 6. Honolulu

Green, R.C., 1980. *Makaha Before 1880 A.D. Makaha Valley Historical Project — Summary. Report 5.* Pacific Anthropological Records 31. Honolulu, Department of Anthropology, Bernice P. Bishop Museum.

Grune, A., 1993. Archeological Synthesis of Waikiki Ahupua'a Focusing on Manoa Valley, 'Ili of Waikiki, Waikiki, Island of O'ahu, Hawai'i. Manuscript, State Historic Preservation Division, Honolulu.

Gunness, J.L., 1993. The Kualoa Archaeological Research Project, 1975-1985: A brief overview. *Hawaiian Archaeology*, 2:50-71.

Hammatt, H., D. Borthwick and D. Shideler, 1985. Archaeological Coring and Testing at Nu'upia Ponds: Kane'ohe Marine Corps Air Station, Mokapu, O'ahu. Manuscript, Cultural Surveys Hawaii, Kailua.

Hammatt, H. and D. Shideler, 1991. Archaeological Disinterment of Inadvertent Finds at Site 50-80-14-4266 on Dole Street, Kanewai, Manoa, Kona District, O'ahu. Manuscript, Cultural Surveys Hawaii, Kailua.

Hammatt, H., D. Shideler, R. Chiogioji and R. Scoville, 1990. Sediment Coring in Kawainui Marsh, Kailua, O'ahu, Ko'olaupoko. Manuscript, Cultural Surveys Hawaii, Kailua.

Handy, E.S.C. and E. Handy, 1972. *Native Planters in Old Hawaii: Their Life, Lore, and Environment.* Bernice P. Bishop Museum Bulletin 233. Honolulu.

Haun, A., 1985. An Archaeological Survey of the Naval Magazine and Naval Communications Area Transmission Facility, Lualualei, O'ahu, Hawai'i. Manuscript, Department of Anthropology, Bernice P. Bishop Museum, Honolulu (O-1122).

Hawaiian Studies Institute, 1987. *Map: O'ahu Pre-Māhele Moku and Ahupua'a.* Honolulu, Kamehameha Schools.

Henry, J. and P. Rosendahl, 1993. Archaeological Inventory Survey, Waiawa Floodplain Feasibility Study Project Area. Land of Manana, 'Ewa District, Island of Oahu. Manuscript, PHRI, Hilo.

Hommon, R.J., 1976. The Formation of Primitive States in Pre-Contact Hawaii. Unpublished Ph.D. dissertation, University of Arizona, Tucson.

—— 1980. National Register of Historic Places Multiple Resource Nomination Form for the Historic Resources of Kaho'olawe. Manuscript, State Historic Preservation Division, Honolulu.

—— 1986. Social evolution in ancient Hawaii. In P.V. Kirch (ed.), *Island Societies: Archaeological Approaches to Evolution and Transformation*, pp.55-68. Cambridge, Cambridge University Press.

—— 1992a. The view from out on a limb, or confessions of a generalist. *New Zealand Journal of Archaeology*, 14:151-58.

—— 1992b. The butterfly effect in ancient Hawaii. Paper presented at the 5th Conference on Hawaiian Archaeology. Kaua'i Community College, 28 March 1992.

Hunt, T.L. and R.M. Holsen, 1991. An early radiocarbon chronology for the Hawaiian Islands: A preliminary analysis. *Asian Perspectives*, 30:147-61.

I'i, J.P., 1959. *Fragments of Hawaiian History*. Honolulu, Bishop Museum Press.

Kamakau, S.M., 1961. *Ruling Chiefs of Hawaii*. Honolulu, Kamehameha Schools Press.

—— 1964. *Ka Po'e Kahiko: The People of Old*. Bernice P. Bishop Museum Special Publication 51. Honolulu, Bishop Museum Press.

—— 1976. *The Works of the People of Old: Na Hana a ka Po'e Kahiko*. Bernice P. Bishop Museum Special Publication 61. Honolulu, Bishop Museum Press.

—— 1991. *Tales and Traditions of the People of Old: Na Mo'olelo a ka Po'e Kahiko*. Honolulu, Bishop Museum Press.

Kame'eleihiwa, L., 1986. Land and the Promise of Capitalism: A Dilemma for the Hawaiian Chiefs of the 1848 Mahele. Unpublished Ph.D. dissertation, University of Hawaii at Manoa.

Kelly, M., 1985. Notes on the history of Lualualei. In A. Haun, An Archaeological Survey of the Naval Magazine and Naval Communications Area Transmission Facility, Lualualei, O'ahu, Hawai'i, pp. 310-48. Manuscript, Department of Anthropology, Bernice P. Bishop Museum, Honolulu (O-1122).

—— 1989. Dynamics of production intensification in Precontact Hawaii. In S. van der Leeuw and R. Torrence (eds), *What's New? A Closer Look at the Process of Innovation*, pp.82-106. London, Unwin Hyman.

Kelly, M. and B. Nakamura, 1981. Historical Study of Kawainui Marsh Area, Island of O'ahu. Manuscript, Department of Anthropology, Bernice P. Bishop Museum, Honolulu (O-155).

Kikuchi, W.K., 1973. Hawaiian Aquacultural Systems. Unpublished Ph.D. thesis, University of Arizona, Tucson.

Kirch, P.V., 1973. Early Settlements and Initial Adaptational Modes in the Hawaiian Islands. Paper presented at the Annual Meeting of the Society for American Anthropology, San Francisco.

—— 1974. The chronology of early Hawaiian settlement. *Archaeology and Physical Anthropology in Oceania*, 9:110-19.

—— 1984. *The Evolution of the Polynesian Chiefdoms*. Cambridge, Cambridge University Press.

—— 1985. *Feathered Gods and Fishhooks: An Introduction to Hawaiian Archaeology and Prehistory*. Honolulu, University of Hawaii Press.

Kirch, P.V. and M. Spriggs, 1993. A radiocarbon chronology for the upper Anahulu Valley, O'ahu. *Hawaiian Archaeology*, 2:4-9.

Kolb, M., 1991. Social Power, Chiefly Authority, and Ceremonial Architecture in an Island Polity, Maui, Hawaii. Unpublished Ph.D. dissertation, University of California at Los Angeles.

—— 1994. Ritual activity and chiefly economy at an upland religious site on Maui, Hawai'i. *Journal of Field Archaeology*, 21:417-36.

Kolb, M., P.J. Conte, M. McFadden and C. Mitchell, n.d. Archaeological Survey and Excavations at Pahe'ehe'e Ridge, Wai'anae Ahupua'a, Wai'anae District, Island of O'ahu. Draft Manuscript, State Historic Preservation Division, Honolulu.

Kolb, M., C. Mitchell, P.J. Conte and M. McFadden, 1993. Archaeological Inventory Survey in Kalawahine 'Ili, Honolulu Ahupua'a, Kona District, Island of O'ahu. Manuscript, State Historic Preservation Division, Honolulu.

Ladd, E.J., 1969. 'Alealea Temple Site, Honaunau: Salvage Report. In R. Pearson (ed.), *Archaeology on the Island of Hawaii*. Asian and Pacific Archaeology Series, 3:95-130. Honolulu, Social Science Research Institute, University of Hawaii.

—— 1973. Kaneaki temple site — an excavation report. In E.J. Ladd (ed.), *Makaha Valley Historical Project: Interim Report 4*. Pacific Anthropological Records 19:1-30. Honolulu, Department of Anthropology, Bernice P. Bishop Museum.

—— 1987. *Excavations at Site A-27. Archaeology at Pu'uhonua o Honaunau National Historical Park*. Western Archaeological and Conservation Center Publications in Anthropology 43. Tucson.

Macdonald, G. and A. Abbott, 1970. *Volcanoes in the Sea: The Geology of Hawaii*. Honolulu, University Press of Hawaii.

Malo, D., n.d. He Buke no ka 'Oihana Kula. Manuscript, State Historic Preservation Division, Honolulu.

McAllister, J.G., 1933. *Archaeology of Oahu*. Bernice P. Bishop Museum Bulletin 104. Honolulu.

McDermott, M., 1992. Proposed Research and Management Strategies for the Cultural Resources of the Ahupua'a of Waikele, District of 'Ewa, Island of O'ahu. Manuscript, State Historic Preservation Division, Honolulu.

Menzies, A., 1920. *Hawaii Nei 128 Years Ago: Journal of Archibald Menzies, Kept During His Three Visits to the Sandwich or Hawaiian Islands when*

Acting as Surgeon and Naturalist on Board HMS Discovery. Honolulu, The New Freedom Press.

Miller, L., 1989. Archaeological Monitoring of the Tinker Road Bridge Repair (Replacement) Project, Bellows Air Force Station, Waimanalo, O'ahu Island, Hawai'i. Manuscript, Department of Anthropology, Bernice P. Bishop Museum, Honolulu.

Mills, P. and S. Williams, 1992. Draft: Archaeological Investigations in the Luluku Banana Farmers' Relocation Area, Maunawili Valley, Kailua Ahupua'a, O'ahu. Manuscript, Department of Anthropology, Bernice P. Bishop Museum, Honolulu (O-991).

The Nature Conservancy of Hawaii, 1987. Biological Database and Reconnaissance Survey of Nanakuli. Manuscript, The Nature Conservancy of Hawaii, Honolulu.

Nettles, B., 1992. Kane'ohe. Manuscript, State Historic Preservation Division, Honolulu.

Newman, T.S., 1972. Man in the prehistoric Hawaiian ecosystem. In E.A. Kay (ed.), *A Natural History of the Hawaiian Islands: Selected Readings*, pp.559-603. Honolulu, University Press of Hawaii.

Ogata, C., 1992. Settlement Survey of Wailupe 'Ili, Waikiki Ahupua'a, Kona District, Island of O'ahu. Manuscript, State Historic Preservation Division, Honolulu.

Ono, C., 1992. A Synthesis of Nu'uanu Valley, Honolulu Ahupua'a, Kona, Oahu. Manuscript, State Historic Preservation Division, Honolulu.

Pearson, R.J., P.V. Kirch and M. Pietrusewsky, 1971. An early prehistoric site at Bellows Beach, Waimanalo, Oahu, Hawaiian Islands. *Archaeology and Physical Anthropology in Oceania*, 6:204-34.

Riesenberg, S., 1968. *The Native Polity of Ponape*. Smithsonian Contributions to Anthropology 10. Washington, D.C.

Rosendahl, P.H., A. Haun, J. Halbig, M. Kaschko and M. Allen, 1987. Kahoolawe Excavations, 1982-83. Data Recovery Project, Island of Kahoolawe, Hawaii. Manuscript, PHRI, Hilo.

Sahlins, M.D., 1971. An Interdisciplinary Investigation of Hawaiian Social Morphology and Economy in the Late Prehistoric and Early Historic Periods. Grant proposal to NSF. Manuscript, State Historic Preservation Division, Honolulu.

—— 1973. Historical Anthropology of the Hawaiian Kingdom. Proposal to NSF. Manuscript, State Historic Preservation Division, Honolulu.

—— 1992. *Anahulu: The Anthropology of History in the Kingdom of Hawaii. Volume One: Historical Ethnography*. Chicago, University of Chicago Press.

Schilt, A., 1991. Archaeological Literature and Archival Review, Moiliili and Waikiki Districts, Honolulu. Manuscript, ERC Environmental and Energy Services Co., Honolulu (O-822).

Schmitt, R., 1971. New estimates of the pre-censal population of Hawaii. *Journal of the Polynesian Society*, 80:237-43.

—— 1973. *The Missionary Censuses of Hawaii*. Pacific Anthropological Records 20. Honolulu, Department of Anthropology, Bernice P. Bishop Museum.

Scott-Cummings, L., 1991. Pollen Findings in Nanakuli Valley, O'ahu. Manuscript, State Historic Preservation Division, Honolulu.

Shun, K., 1992. Draft: Archaeological Monitoring and Sampling During Installation of Perimeter Security Fencing, Bellows Air Force Station, Waimanalo, Koolaupoko District, Island of Oahu, Hawaii. Manuscript, Archaeological Associates Oceania, Kane'ohe.

Spear, R., 1991. Draft: Preliminary Report on the Archaeology of the Access Road Corridor in North Halawa Valley, O'ahu Island, Hawai'i. Manuscript, Department of Anthropology, Bernice P. Bishop Museum, Honolulu (O-1110).

Spriggs, M.J.T., 1988. The Hawaiian transformation of Ancestral Polynesian society: Conceptualizing chiefly states. In J. Gledhill, B. Bender and M.T. Larsen (eds), *State and Society*, pp.57-73. London, Unwin Hyman.

Spriggs, M. and A. Anderson, 1993. Late colonization of East Polynesia. *Antiquity*, 67:200-17.

Stannard, D., 1989. *Before the Horror: The Population of Hawai'i on the Eve of Western Contact*. Honolulu, Social Science Research Institute, University of Hawaii.

Stearns, H., 1966. *Geology of the State of Hawaii*. Palo Alto, Pacific Books.

Stearns, H. and K. Vaksvik, 1935. *Geology and Ground-Water Resources of the Island of Oahu, Hawaii*. Bulletin 1. Wailuku, Division of Hydrography, Territory of Hawaii.

Stokes, J.F.G., 1933. New bases for Hawaiian chronology. *41st Annual Report of the Hawaiian Historical Society for the Year 1932*, pp.23-65. Honolulu.

Streck, C. and F. Watanabe, 1988. Archaeological Reconnaissance of Areas Proposed for Emergency Flood Control Repair and Replacement of Structures, Bellows Air Force Station (BAFS), Waimanalo District, Oahu Island. Manuscript, U.S. Army Corps of Engineers, Fort Shafter, Honolulu.

Thrum, T., 1907. *Heiaus* and *heiau* sites throughout the Hawaiian Islands. *The Hawaiian Annual for 1907*, pp.36-48. Honolulu.

Tomonari-Tuggle, M., 1981. North Kohala: A Perception of a Changing Community. Manuscript, State Historic Preservation Division, Honolulu (H-265).

—— 1989. *An Archaeological Reconnaissance Survey: Na Pali Coast State Park, Island of Kaua'i.* Honolulu, Historic Sites Section, Division of State Parks.

Tuggle, H.D., 1979. Hawaii. In J. Jennings (ed.), *The Prehistory of Polynesia*, pp.167-99. Cambridge, Harvard University Press.

Tuggle, H.D., R. Cordy and M. Child, 1978. Volcanic glass hydration-rind age determinations for Bellows Dune, Hawaii. *New Zealand Archaeological Association Newsletter*, 21:58-77.

Vancouver, G., 1798. *A Voyage of Discovery to the North Pacific Ocean and Round the World.* 3 vols. London, for G.G. and J. Robinson and J. Edwards.

Walker, A., A. Haun and P. Rosendahl, 1988. Intensive Survey and Test Excavations, Site 50-OA-2911, Kahuku Point Archaeological Area, Kuilima Resort Expansion Project. Manuscript, PHRI, Hilo (O-580).

Watanabe, F., 1986. Archaeological Site Survey and Subsurface Testing for the FY89 Chapel Center Facility and Daycare Center, Fort Shafter. Manuscript, U.S. Army Corps of Engineers, Fort Shafter, Honolulu (O-553).

Wickler, S., J.S. Athens and J. Ward, 1991. Draft Vegetation and Landscape Change in a Leeward Coastal Environment, Paleoenvironmental and Archaeological Investigations, Fort Shafter Flats Sewerline Project, Honolulu, Hawai'i. Manuscript, International Archaeological Research Institute Inc., Honolulu (O-793).

Williams, S., 1989. A Preliminary Report of Test Excavations on Sites 50-OA-G5-106 and G5-110, Luluku, Kane'ohe, Ko'olaupoko, O'ahu. Manuscript, Department of Anthropology, Bernice P. Bishop Museum, Honolulu (O-663).

—— 1992. Early inland settlement expansion and the effect of geomorphological change on the archaeological record in K_ne'ohe, O'ahu. *New Zealand Journal of Archaeology*, 14:67-78.

Yen, D.E., P.V. Kirch, P. Rosendahl and T. Riley, 1972. Prehistoric agriculture in the upper valley of Makaha, Oahu. In E.J. Ladd and D.E. Yen (eds), *Makaha Valley Historical Project: Interim Report 3*. Pacific Anthropological Records 18:59-94. Honolulu, Department of Anthropology, Bernice P. Bishop Museum.